Ancient Cyprus

VERONICA TATTON-BROWN

Published for
The Trustees of the British Museum by
BRITISH MUSEUM PUBLICATIONS

To my parents

THE TRUSTEES OF THE BRITISH MUSEUM
acknowledge with gratitude the generosity of
THE A. G. LEVENTIS FOUNDATION
for the grant which made possible the
publication of this book.

Published by British Museum Publications
46 Bloomsbury Street, London WC1B 3QQ

Designed by Roger Davies
Phototypeset in Photina by Southern Positives
and Negatives (SPAN), Lingfield, Surrey
Origination by Colourscan, Singapore
Printed in Italy by New Interlitho

Front cover Upper part of a colossal limestone
statue of a bearded man, a worshipper or priest
of Apollo or perhaps even the god himself. He is
dressed in Greek fashion in a *chiton* (short-
sleeved tunic) and a *himation* (cloak). From the
sanctuary of Apollo at Idalion, *c*.490–80 BC.
Ht 104.0 cm.

Back cover Bronze statuette representing the
protector, perhaps divine, of the copper
industry. He wears a horned helmet, carries a
shield and spear and stands on an ingot shaped
like an ox-hide. From the 'sanctuary of the
Ingot god' at Enkomi, 12th century BC.
Ht 35 cm.

Inside front cover Pair of gold-plated bronze
spiral rings for the ears or hair, ending in
horned griffin heads with enamel and filigree
decoration. This type of spiral ring was a
Cypriot speciality and this particular material
favoured by Cypriot jewellers. From Amathus,
5th century BC. L 3.5 cm.

Title page Vase in the form of a bull, made of
Base Ring ware with white painted decoration.
From Maroni, 1400–1200 BC. L 16 cm.

This page View of the northern part of the city
of Salamis with remains of public buildings of
the Roman period. In the centre the
gymnasium with a colonnaded *palaestra*
(wrestling ground) and a bath building on its
seaward side.

Contents

Preface

This book is intended to serve as a handbook to the permanent exhibition of Cypriot antiquities in the British Museum, known as the 'A. G. Leventis Gallery of Cypriot Antiquities', since it was made possible by a grant from the A. G. Leventis Foundation in 1987. The A. G. Leventis Foundation has also generously supported this publication.

Like the exhibition, the book surveys the civilisation of ancient Cyprus by looking at different aspects. This thematic treatment was originally suggested by the Australian scholar and diplomat Dr Robert Merrillees as being particularly suited to a museum collection such as ours. The British Museum is indeed fortunate in possessing one of the largest collections of Cypriot antiquities outside Cyprus itself. Its acquisition was described by B. F. Cook in his preface to *Cypriote Art in the British Museum*, but since that book is now out of print, and, more importantly, as this handbook introduces a new permanent gallery, the salient points are repeated here.

The first Cypriot material to enter the collections of the British Museum were coins, which came with the bequest of the collection of the noted antiquary, Richard Payne Knight, in 1824. Coins continued to accumulate, but in 1852 eight stone sculptures, twenty terracottas and an inscription collected in Larnaca were bought from Henry Christy, the banker and ethnologist who bequeathed his collection to the Museum in 1865. In 1866 D. E. Colnaghi, British Consul in Cyprus, presented over three hundred terracottas from different sites, which constitute the first important gift of Cypriot material. Among those who conducted unofficial excavations in the island in the final years of the Turkish administration was Robert (later Sir Robert) Hamilton Lang, a Scotsman and employee of the Ottoman Bank. In 1872 the Museum purchased a large number of stone statues together with some statuettes of terracotta and bronze from his excavations in the sanctuary of Apollo at Idalion. Lang's superb collection of coins, including two important hoards from Idalion, were acquired by the British Museum between 1871 and 1902.

Another of these 'unofficial excavators' was General Luigi Palma di Cesnola, who, during his term as American (and Russian) consul, explored extensively. The major part of his fine collection was acquired by the Metropolitan Museum of Art in New York, but in 1871 and 1876 the British Museum bought from him over a hundred items of pottery, bronze and terracotta. Unfortunately the exact find-spot of individual pieces is unknown. A fine collection, mainly of bronze tools and weapons of the Early and Middle Bronze Age, was presented by Augustus Woollaston Franks (later Sir Augustus), Keeper of British and Medieval Antiquities, between 1871 and 1883.

Restrictions on unofficial excavations were imposed by the British in 1878, when they took over the administration of Cyprus from the Turks. A German, Max Ohnefalsch Richter, was among the first to carry out official excavations. In 1883 the British Museum acquired terracottas and some stone statuettes from his investigations in the sanctuary of Artemis at Achna. Other antiquities provided by him include Early and Middle Bronze Age pottery from Phoenikiais (Yeri) and Hellenistic and Roman material from Salamis and Kition. His excavations at Phrangissa, Tamassos, in 1885 were paid for by Colonel Falkland Warren. On Warren's death the Museum purchased some interesting inscriptions and fine statues of terracotta and stone.

In 1887 a learned society, the Cyprus Exploration Fund, was formed in London to promote interest in the island. One of the first sites explored under the Fund's auspices was the famed sanctuary of Aphrodite at Old Paphos, and in 1888 the British Museum was presented with some of the finds. In 1891 the

Museum received material from excavations at Salamis carried out the previous year. This was followed by Classical and Hellenistic artefacts from Marion.

The British Museum itself began to excavate in Cyprus in 1893. Between 1893 and 1896 the excavations were financed by funds bequeathed to the Museum by Miss E. T. Turner. Cemeteries at Amathus (1893–4), Kourion (1895) and Enkomi (1896) yielded quantities of pottery and items of stone, terracotta, bronze, glass, faience, ivory and precious metals. By agreement with the authorities in Cyprus, one third of the finds were deposited in the Cyprus Museum, the rest being brought to London. Tomb-groups were kept together.

Further excavations were carried out by the British Museum at the end of the nineteenth century. The Late Bronze Age cemeteries at Maroni, Hala Sultan Tekké and Klavdia were investigated between 1897 and 1899. A smaller excavation of tombs at Kouklia (Old Paphos) yielded some Iron Age as well as Bronze Age material.

The catalogue of the coins of Cyprus in the British Museum was published in 1904, and in the twentieth century the collection has been enlarged, principally by various gifts and purchases. Some Bronze Age Cypriot weapons were among the items from the part of Canon Greenwell's collection that was bought and then donated to the Museum by the American millionaire J. Pierpont Morgan in 1909. In 1939 and 1940 the Museum purchased some Early Bronze Age tomb-groups from Vounous excavated by J. R. Stewart of the University of Melbourne (Australia). In recent years the Department of Antiquities of Cyprus has generously allowed the Museum to acquire sherds of pottery from surveys conducted by the British Lemba Archaeological Project and by the Swiss-German expedition at Old Paphos. The largest acquisition of this century to date is the group of material which was transferred from the Victoria and Albert Museum, South Kensington, in 1980. The majority of the items come from excavations organised by Horatio Kitchener (later Lord Kitchener of

Map of the Mediterranean and the Near East

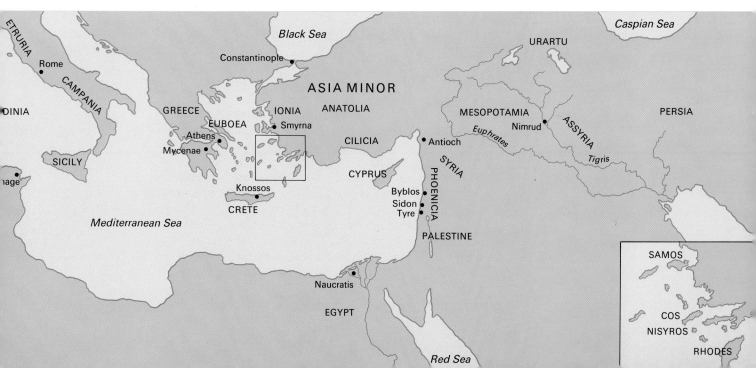

Khartoum), who was then director of a survey of Cyprus, and carried out by George Gordon Hake at Salamis, Kourion and Gastria (Alaas) in 1883. This transfer also included additions to our Cesnola collection.

A collection acquired in this way cannot be comprehensive. The Museum, for example, has no mosaics or wall-paintings and very few items of the earliest prehistoric phases. This survey attempts to illustrate the civilisation of ancient Cyprus from the Museum's collection and therefore certain aspects like domestic and public architecture and town planning receive little or no attention. Nonetheless, much of the Cypriot material is of the highest quality and interest and the generosity of the A. G. Leventis Foundation has made it available to a wider public.

1 The natural history of Cyprus

1 View of the Troodos mountains from near the monastery of Panayia Khrysorroyiatissa (Our Lady of the Golden Pomegranate).

The climate and vegetation of Cyprus are typically Mediterranean. The landscape is dominated by mountains, the Kyrenia range in the north and the Troodos massif in the south. Between the two lies a large central plain. A typical feature is the thick hard deposit of *havara* or *kafkalla* (broadly translatable as limestone), sometimes overlying a layer of *terra rossa* (red soil) on the plateaux and ridges. There are perennial fresh water springs at Lapithos and Kythrea in the north, but apart from these and certain streams in or from the Troodos massif there are no rivers which are free-flowing all the year round. The major rivers, with their rough stony beds, are dry in summer but flow torrentially, breaking their banks, in winter. The rainfall in antiquity may have been higher, but it is likely that as today the continuous supply of fresh water was limited and unreliable, since it would have depended on the snowfall in the Troodos and the rainfall elsewhere on the island.

Our information about the land in antiquity, before its modification by human effort, and the plant and animal life it supported comes from the analysis of pollen, botanical remains and bones from archaeological excavations, representations in art and the occasional written record. Chief among the literary sources is an anecdote recorded by Strabo in the first century AD and attributed to his fellow geographer Eratosthenes of the second century BC. He tells that authorisation was given to any inhabitant to cut down as many trees as he could and keep the cleared land as his own property tax-free. The countryside was covered by thick forests which hampered cultivation, and the activities of the timber-cutters requiring fuel for copper-smelting or ship-building timber had failed to clear enough land. The wealth of the island was legendary. 'Cyprus is second to none of the islands of the Mediterranean: it is rich in wine and oil, produces grain in abundance and possesses extensive copper mines at Tamassos', wrote Strabo in AD 23.

The lowlands, comprising the central plain and the strip of land around the coast, were made up of marshlands and rich fertile meadows. Many weeds grow in these areas today and several of these species have been identified in Late Bronze Age contexts. Seed remains show that wheat and barley were cultivated by early settlers, and gold beads in the shape of grains of wheat form parts of necklaces of the later second millennium. Date palms and poppies were also grown by the early inhabitants. The date palm in part inspired representations of the 'tree of life' and the palmette, and palm trees are also among the motifs decorating funerary mouthpieces and diadems made between 1400 and 1200 BC. The opium poppy may be the inspiration behind the form of a particular type of juglet made in Base Ring Ware between about 1650 and 1400 BC and exported to Egypt, Syria and Palestine. It has been suggested that such jugs contained opium, a theory that has been upheld by the analysis of the surviving contents of some but not all. Opium can probably therefore be numbered among Cyprus' exports at this time. Laurel, one of many shrubs, was an important component of the wreaths regularly worn from the late sixth century BC onwards, as the statues show; some carry laurel branches from a slightly earlier date.

The dense forests that covered the uplands – the whole of the Kyrenia mountain range and the lower slopes of Troodos – contained the Aleppo pine of Cyprus, the cedar and the cypress. All of these except the cedar (known from the fifth century BC onwards) have been identified in prehistoric contexts (before 1050 BC). The pine is the species mentioned by Theophrastus in the fourth century BC as one of the chief forest trees used for ship-building. The olive, also indigenous, flourished throughout the hills and here too grew trees laden with

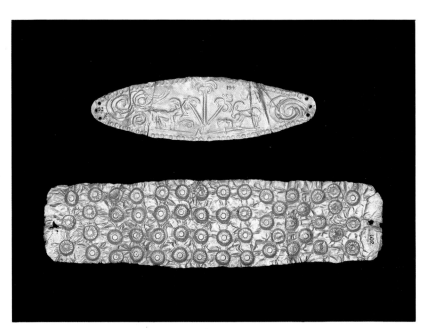

fruit and nuts, notably pomegranates, figs, almonds and pistachios. The carob was probably introduced from the Yemen in the second century AD. Vines grew on the south-facing slopes of Troodos but on the higher peaks, above 1200 metres, the oak and the Troodos pine predominated. Arrow-like patterns, which may represent conifers, and the occasional stylised but more realistic tree appear on painted vases of the later eighth and seventh centuries BC, but these apart the tree is seldom represented before the fifth century. Thereafter there are some accurate portrayals of trees, some of which bear fruit. A fine illustration of the grape harvest appears on one of the mosaics of around AD 200 in the house of Dionysos at New Paphos.

The fruit most often depicted from an early date was the pomegranate, which with its numerous seeds may have been a symbol of fertility. The glass examples of the fourteenth to twelfth centuries BC, with their pointed calyx tips and short necks, are faithful representations of the fruit, unlike the contemporary Egyptian version. Gold pendants in the form of pomegranates also date from the Late Bronze Age and pomegranates made of pottery decorate ring vases of the late second and early first millennia, while in the Iron Age they are made into children's rattles.

The rosette is one of the motifs that decorate funerary diadems and mouthpieces of gold in the Late Bronze Age, but it enjoyed its greatest popularity on painted vases from the beginning of the Iron Age until the sixth century BC and on stone reliefs of later dates, appearing in a number of forms. There is no reason to believe that it had any deep significance, and it is best seen as a purely decorative motif originally inspired by the designs on Syrian and Phoenician minor works of art and textiles. The lotus is another favourite plant motif, of vase-painters during the earlier Iron Age but it appears too on the decorated metal

bowls and other artefacts evidently made in Cyprus by resident Phoenician craftsmen or under strong north Syrian influence. Its origin, therefore, is not hard to find. Indeed, an earlier appearance is on a vessel of about 1600 BC made in a fabric of eastern inspiration, wheel-made Bichrome Ware. The flower itself is the Egyptian water-lily of the Nile (lotus nymphaea) and the Egyptian depictions, which have three outer petals with the spaces filled with a varying number of smaller petals, are the truest representations. As a motif it appeared in the east in the earlier second millennium, where a rather more stylised 'north Syrian' version with two outer and one inner petal had been developed by the Iron Age. Many varieties of these two principal versions decorate Near Eastern ivories of the earlier first millennium, and the Cypriot artists are similarly ingenious. The lily, together with the date palm and lotus, is the inspiration behind the many representations of the 'tree of life' in Cypriot art, which are generally of eastern origin. The Greek version of the palmette is borrowed by artists mainly from the fifth century BC onwards, and of Greek origin also are the ivy leaf and acanthus which appear in Cypriot art from about the same time.

Ten species of wild animals have been identified as native to Cyprus and of these the bones of the moufflon (wild sheep), Persian fallow deer, wild pig, hare and fox have been found on prehistoric sites. A mosaic floor of around AD 200 in the atrium of the house of Dionysos at New Paphos shows hunting scenes; among the conventional animals of the hunt are two moufflon, which must have been included to give local colour. The wild pig also appears in these scenes, but earlier portrayals by Cypriot artists include the occasional painted version on vases of the late eighth and early seventh centuries BC, terracotta models of the sixth century and a fine representation in relief on a limestone sarco-

4 A moufflon followed by a hunting dog in a hunting scene on a mosaic of *c.* AD 200 in the eastern portico of the *atrium* (courtyard) of the house of Dionysos at New Paphos.

phagus of about 470–460 BC. The hedgehog, another indigenous species, is perhaps represented by a terracotta model of the thirteenth century BC imported from Greece. Lyre boxes were made of tortoise shells in the Iron Age.

With the first settlers came domesticated animals, including another species of pig, as well as goats, sheep, dogs and cats. Cattle were apparently unknown before the second half of the second millennium and first appear in Cypriot art about 1900 BC. Thereafter it is the bull that receives most attention by artists, and it may have had a religious significance. Bulls' heads were set up on sticks like totem poles and bull-masks were worn by priests (and perhaps worshippers) in religious ceremonies. Models of terracotta, some made into vases, and earrings of gold wire threaded with bulls' heads were made in the Bronze Age, and the bull was a favourite motif among vase painters of the later eighth and seventh centuries BC. The cattle of Geryon, captured by the hero Herakles, represented on a fine limestone relief of the second quarter of the fifth century BC, have humped backs and show a single horn, like the bull which appears with the boar on the limestone sarcophagus (above). Oxen seem to have been used as draught animals in

46a

80

prehistoric times, a practice continued by the Romans. Remains of true horses have been found in contexts from about 1600 BC. Earlier equid bones are most probably those of donkeys or asses, which evidently acted as pack and draught animals, a role they played in later times as well. In the Iron Age lifelike horses are portrayed being ridden or drawing chariots. The terracotta models and painted vases of the Archaic period are again important sources of information about animal life and the way it is represented in Cypriot art. Goats, stags and pigs are all portrayed. The goat and stag also appear on coins of the city–

kingdoms, as does the ram. The terracotta children's rattles in the form of pigs of the Hellenistic and early Roman periods probably portray the domesticated rather than the wild species. Though certainly the home of the poisonous Levant viper, Cyprus seems hardly to have justified the title of Ophioussa (abode of snakes) which she acquired in late antiquity. Snakes figure in art from an early date and are usually associated with the underworld (chthonic) deities. The Egyptian cobra (Uraeus) is adopted as a decorative motif from about the eighth century BC, orginally perhaps reaching Cyprus by way of Syria and Phoenicia, al-

5 Group of terracotta figurines: a pig, a stag and a bird. From Amathus and Kourion, 7th–6th century BC. Ht (of bird) 8.4 cm.

77

6

6 (*Far left*) Snakes and coils decorating a jug of Base Ring ware. From Maroni, 1650–1550 BC. Ht 27.4 cm.

7 (*Left*) Bichrome ware jug decorated with an aquatic-looking bird in the 'free-field' pictorial style characteristic of southern and eastern Cyprus in the Archaic period; *c.*700 BC. Ht 18.0 cm.

though more direct influence may account for its appearance on the Egyptian crowns of some statues and statuettes.

The really fierce wild animals, like tigers, panthers and lions, were not known in Cyprus. Of these the lion is most commonly portrayed and must, like the representations of mythological beasts, owe much to outside contact and influence. In general these images were initially influenced by the work of Cyprus' eastern neighbours, notably in Syria and Phoenicia, which was also the source of the Egyptian features. From about the fifth century BC the representations usually show increasing dependence on Greek models.

Cyprus, being on the migration routes between Europe and Africa and Asia, is host to a great number of birds. The only indigenous species is the Cyprus warbler, but quite a few sub-species, including several songbirds, are also native to the island. Most conspicuous among the winter visitors today are aquatic birds, like ducks, cranes, geese, swans, flamingoes, and songbirds including starlings, thrushes, larks and blackbirds. Eagles and vultures breed, and in the spring the nightingale arrives.

Few remains of birds have survived from antiquity and the representations in art, though common, are often not specific. However, it seems that then, as now, vultures and eagles inhabited the mountainous regions, whereas ducks, swans, doves, partridges and songbirds were found in the fertile lowlands and marshlands.

Like the remains of birds, those of fish have seldom survived. Unlike birds, however, fish played an insignificant role in the artist's repertoire, except in the Archaic period when they are portrayed on some painted vases with pictorial scenes.

2 The historical background

The first evidence for human occupation in Cyprus is some time before 7000 BC, comparatively late in comparison with that of her neighbours in Anatolia (Asia Minor) to the north, and Syria and Palestine to the east. The earliest settlers probably arrived from the Syro-Palestinian coast. They chose sites which were often conspicuous landmarks, with good arable land and an adequate water supply. Most were either on the coast or in river valleys with easy access to the sea. The communities were fairly scattered, mainly along the north coast and in the south. The economy was based on mixed farming, fishing or hunting, but pottery was not used. The

culture, which takes its name from the best-known site of the period, Khirokitia, near the south coast, was short-lived. It seems to have gone into a decline, to be finally extinguished around 6000 BC. This was followed by a period of about fifteen hundred years during which the island seems to have been almost completely deserted.

The second group of inhabitants had no connections with their predecessors, although they sometimes occupied the same sites. The culture is called after the extensively explored site of Sotira in the south. The people lived in agricultural villages which were comparatively short-lived; they maintained contact

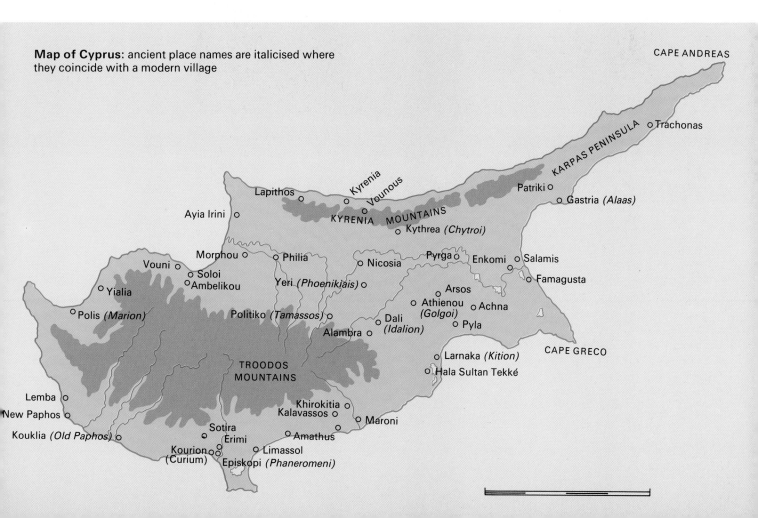

Map of Cyprus: ancient place names are italicised where they coincide with a modern village

with each other but not with the outside world. The demise of this culture appears to have been rapid, perhaps precipitated at least in some places by an earthquake, and several sites were abandoned.

The population of the succeeding Chalcolithic period (literally, copper-stone age) was not entirely new. The western end of the island was now more densely settled, and there were important innovations. Metal was used, though it was still uncommon, and a new type of miniature sculpture was produced. Towards the end of the period new burial customs were practised, foreshadowing those of the Bronze Age. Around 2500 BC momentous changes took place in the north, which even now are not fully understood. Here the metalwork and pottery shows strong affinities with that of southern Anatolia. It may be that refugees arrived from that area, fleeing from catastrophes that had befallen them around 2700/2600 BC. It is clear, however, that these changes did not occur throughout the island at the same time, but were initially concentrated at sites in the river valleys of the north-western central plain.

34

9 (*Far left*) Wheel-made jug decorated in red and black with birds and geometric motifs. One of a group of vessels which look distinctly Palestinian but whose shapes and linear ornaments mirror those of Cypriot White Painted ware. This Bichrome Wheel-Made ware was produced in short-lived workshops in eastern Cyprus in the sixteenth century BC. From Maroni. Ht 21 cm.

8 (*Left*) Limestone female figurine whose arms and legs are mere stumps. She is the largest example of this type known at present (36 cm tall) and the material is also unusual. Found in the debris of a destroyed building at Lemba-Lakkous, she is known as the 'Lemba Lady'. She must have been a fertility charm and may even represent a goddess; c.2500 BC.

10 (*Right*) An imported Mycenaean Greek silver bowl. The handle is not a true 'wishbone' and is therefore unlike those of contemporary Cypriot pottery vessels. Parallels for the shape can be found in Mycenaean bronzework. From Enkomi, 1400–1200 BC. D 20.7 cm.

Nevertheless Early Bronze Age culture quite soon spread throughout the island. The availability of water and agricultural land still dictated the choice of sites. The transition to the Middle Bronze Age, around 1900 BC, was marked by no great upheaval. Except for the most mountainous regions, the whole island was now occupied. Towards the end of the period Cyprus finally came out of her isolation. Goods were imported and Cypriot products reached Egypt and the Near East; society was becoming more urban. In the seventeenth century BC there seems to have been some internal strife, perhaps even a plague, but no major catastrophe befell the whole island.

The Late Bronze Age was a period of great prosperity. Following the establishment of peace in the eastern Mediterranean world around 1500 BC, Cyprus enjoyed close trading contacts with the Near East, Egypt and the Greek world. Life was particularly prosperous in the towns, established mainly on the east and south coasts, often with fine harbours. The island did not escape the disturbances that affected the entire Mediterranean world in the

late thirteenth and early twelfth century BC. Bands of marauders, known as the 'Sea Peoples', were roaming the Mediterranean. and towards 1200 BC most of the principal towns of Mycenaean Greece were destroyed and abandoned. Some sites in Cyprus suffered violent destructions about the same time. The island, however, recovered. Life continued in all the major towns in the twelfth century BC and prosperity returned. The undeniable influence from Mycenaean Greece and Crete on Cypriot pottery, bronzework and sealstones of this time may have been due to the gradual and intermittent arrival of settlers from the Bronze Age Greek world. In other respects, however, the culture remained untouched by Greek influence. The script and burial customs were unchanged; the weight systems continued to mirror those of the Near East and Egypt, and eastern influence is apparent in certain religious customs. Cypriot craftsmen continued to import luxury materials from the east, while their own products showed a blend of Aegean, eastern and Cypriot elements as before. Immigration from the Bronze Age Greek world on

11 Cypriot bronze statuette of a male worshipper. The impetus for the production of such strongly Egyptianising bronze statuettes in Cyprus seems to have come directly during the period of Egyptian rule. From the sanctuary of Apollo at Idalion, c.550 BC. Ht 22 cm.

a larger scale probably happened around 1100 BC. New Mycenaean Greek burial customs were practised in some eleventh-century cemeteries, and the Cypro-Minoan script of the Late Bronze Age died out, to be replaced by Cypro-Syllabic and the Greek language.

By about 1050 BC iron had already been in use in Cyprus for about a century. The two hundred years between 1050 and 850 BC are usually described as a 'Dark Age', but even then contacts were maintained with both east and west, and jewellery and metalwork are evidence of some prosperity. The arrival of the Phoenicians, at least at Kition, in the mid-ninth century BC prompted a revival in Cypriot culture. 'Phoenician' pottery and metalwork were now made locally and Phoenician motifs adopted. There was strong interaction also between Cyprus and the states of North Syria.

The Archaic period (750–475 BC) was marked by a swift succession of foreign overlords; Assyria (c.709–669 BC), Egypt (570/60–545 BC) and Persia (from c.545 BC). Internally the island was organised into autonomous city–kingdoms; seven, and later ten, are mentioned in Assyrian documents. The city–kingdoms grew prosperous and had wide-ranging commercial connections. Towards the end of the sixth century BC they began to strike their own coinage. In 499/8 BC Cyprus joined with the East Greek cities of Ionia in the Ionian Revolt, an attempt to break away from Persian rule. This ended in failure. In the winter of 498/7 BC the cities of Cyprus, which had been holding out, were put to siege and eventually reduced.

Throughout the Classical period (475–325 BC) Cyprus was poised between mainland Greece and Persia. The failure of the Ionian Revolt had left Persia firmly in control. Twenty years later the Cypriot cities were freed by an allied Greek fleet, but Persian rule soon reasserted itself, although the Athenian commander Cimon in 450/449 BC tried once more to secure the island as a Greek base. For forty years from 411 BC Cypriot politics were dominated by Evagoras I of Salamis, who was a great philhellene and openly welcomed all things Greek. By 391 BC, with the help of Athens and Egypt, he controlled a large part of Cyprus. However, Athenian support was lost when, under the Peace of Antalcidas in 386 BC, the Athenians agreed to recognise Persian sovereignty over the cities of Asia and Cyprus. With Egypt as his only ally, Evagoras fought on against the Persians. He was eventually defeated in 381 BC, but negotiated a settlement under which he retained the throne of Salamis, while losing control over the rest of Cyprus. Evagoras I was murdered in 374/3 BC, and in the succeeding years the Cypriot cities fought among themselves, but Evagoras' successors continued the struggle against Persia. In 351 BC the Cypriot cities joined with Phoenicia and Egypt in another revolt against Persia, but this too was suppressed, and by 344/343 BC all the kingdoms of Cyprus were momentarily under Persian control. However, Alexander the Great, King of Macedon and leader of the Greeks, had been gaining considerable successes against the Persian Empire. Following the Greek victory at the Battle of Issus in 333 BC, the Cypriot cities voluntarily submitted to Alexander. More than two hundred years of Persian overall control was finally brought to an end.

Following Alexander's death in 323 BC, his generals, struggling to inherit his empire, used the island as a battleground and a number of the city–kingdoms were destroyed. In 294 BC Cyprus was annexed by Ptolemy, Alexander's general who had claimed Egypt as his share. The city–kingdoms finally ceased to exist and the island became part of the large Hellenistic monarchy of Egypt. For the next two and a half centuries, apart from a short period in the second century BC, Cyprus remained in Ptolemaic hands. The island was organised as a military command under the overall control of a *strategos* (governor-general). All the *strategoi* and the other high officials including the city commandants were non-Cypriots, directly appointed by the king of Egypt. Certain democratic forms of internal administration were introduced, and in the third century BC some minor Phoenician dynasts were tolerated, at least at Lapithos in the north. The Ptolemies themselves were Macedonian Greeks, and so Cyprus became artistically orientated to the Greek (Hellenistic) world. Although the island's natural resources, notably copper, corn and ship-building timber, were exploited for the benefit of the Egyptian kings, in return she enjoyed comparative peace, broken occasionally by attacks from the Seleucid kings of Syria. In 58 BC Cyprus was first annexed by Rome, now a major force in the eastern Mediterranean. During the civil wars of the Roman Republic she was returned to the Ptolemies of Egypt by Julius Caesar, who gave the island to his mistress, Cleopatra VII. In 36 BC the gift was confirmed by Mark Antony, then Cleopatra's husband. However, in 30 BC Octavian, later to be Augustus, the first Roman emperor, took Alexandria, the Egyptian capital. Cleopatra committed suicide, and Cyprus reverted to Rome.

Together with Cilicia on the southern coast of Asia Minor (modern Turkey), the island was at first incorporated in the province of Syria. In 27 BC Cyprus was detached from Syria and became a Senatorial Province. Thereafter, until the reorganisation of the Empire about three hundred years later, the island was ruled by governors of senatorial rank, appointed annually and given the title of Proconsul. Administration was organised in four districts – Paphos in the west, Amathus in the south, Salamis on the east and Lapithos on the north. There were twelve or thirteen cities and Paphos was the capital, as it had been since early in the second century BC. Like the Ptolemies, the Romans exploited the island's natural resources to enrich their own coffers. As part of the Roman east, the civilisation remained basically Greek. In the late third century AD the emperor Diocletian began reorganising the Empire. This process was continued by Constantine the Great, and Cyprus was assigned to the most easterly of the twelve dioceses that were created. In AD 330 Byzantium, renamed Constantinople (modern Istanbul), replaced Rome as the capital of the Roman Empire. On the division of the Roman Empire in AD 395 Cyprus was allocated to the eastern half. This, and the establishment of Christianity as the official religion about the same time, opened a new era in the island's history.

12 (*Left*) Limestone statue of a female lyre-player in Greek dress, with her *chiton* (tunic) girded just below her breasts. Her features resemble those of Berenice I (*c*.340 to before 275 BC), the wife of Ptolemy I, King of Egypt and Cyprus. From the sanctuary of Apollo at Idalion, early 3rd century BC. Ht 55.5 cm.

13 (*Below*) Portrait of the Roman emperor Vespasian (AD 69–79) on a bronze sestertius struck by the *Koinon* of Cypriot cities. The reverse shows Zeus of Salamis (see 71).

3 Island of copper

Cyprus was renowned for copper in antiquity and, indeed, the very word 'copper' comes from the Roman name for the metal *Cyprium aes* (literally 'copper of Cyprus'). The principal copper-bearing ores are on the north and north-east slopes of the Troodos mountains. Less frequently they occur in the southern foothills. Discoveries in the mines at Ambelikou, in the northern foothills to the west of Nicosia, show that here the copper deposits were exploited in the nineteenth century BC. At the same time there was considerable metallurgical activity in the nearby settlement at Aletri. This is, as yet, the first archaeological evidence for copper-mining and metalworking in Cyprus but, as we shall see, an earlier date for these activities is suggested by the quantity of copper and bronze items that were produced in the later second millennium.

At present the earliest metal objects date from soon after 4000 BC and a few more belong to the years between about 3000 and 2500 BC. These are not numerous but nonetheless significant since they indicate a knowledge of metalworking and justify giving the title of Chalcolithic (literally 'copper-stone') to that era. All may be made of native copper, which is found in a pure form on the surface of the earth. The technology that led to their manufacture was probably a local development.

Copper ore must have been mined and then smelted to release the metal to produce the many copper and bronze tools and weapons typical of Cyprus in the Early as well as the Middle Bronze Age. The first of the series were made around 2500 BC. Many early utensils are of arsenical copper (either a natural mixture of arsenic and copper, or the product of deliberate alloying). Although arsenic was poisonous and difficult to use, it was not replaced by tin in Cyprus before the nineteenth century BC. Even after this tin-bronze was not universal. Copper (and not bronze) remained the preferred material for weapons for another three hundred years. Tin probably reached Cyprus via Syria from a source as yet undiscovered. It is still unclear how the Cypriots learnt to make bronze by combining copper with a small amount of arsenic or tin. The answer must lie in the interpretation of the events that ushered in the Cypriot Bronze Age. This new metal technology was perhaps introduced by refugees from Anatolia escaping from the disturbances which marked the end of the Early Bronze II period in that area about 2700/2600 BC.

After a spectacular beginning there is little change in Cypriot metalwork until about 1600 BC, and many of the types even survived for another century and a half. Typical of this early series are weapons with hooked (rat-tail) tangs. The tang was inserted into a handle, the form of which may have been similar to those of the terracotta models. The blade was probably cast in a one-piece mould and then hammered. The same type of weapon appears in many different sizes, and the function of a particular item is usually determined by its size, rather an arbitrary means of classification. Swords, dirks, daggers and spearheads are all represented. Among the tools are axes, chisels, awls, drills and punches. Common are flat wedge-shaped axes, which were cast in one-piece moulds and presumably set in slots on the long axis of the handles. To the Middle Bronze Age (*c*.1900–1650 BC) belong axes of a Near Eastern type with long blades and cylindrical ribbed sockets for the handles. The technical skill required in their manufacture is not otherwise known in Cyprus before the late thirteenth or twelfth century BC. All those found in Cyprus are remarkably like each other and yet slightly different from their eastern prototypes. It therefore seems probable that they were made locally by a foreign smith who perhaps brought the moulds with him. Dress-pins of several varieties have been found, often in pairs, but there is little real evidence to show how they were worn. Those with a hole in the shaft are known as toggle pins. Other personal objects are tweezers and razors.

Excavations have revealed increasing metallurgical activity on settlement sites in the Late Bronze Age. Nearly all the major centres, including Enkomi, Kition, Hala Sultan Tekké, Old Paphos and Maroni, provide evidence for copper-smelting, as do smaller settlements like Alassa near Episkopi. Some like Kalavassos–Ayios Dhimitrios apparently owed their existence to the mining and working of copper. This is the time too of the correspondence between the king of a country referred to as *Alashiya* and the pharaoh. The letters are clay tablets inscribed in the cuneiform (wedge-shaped) script of western Asia and the language is Akkadian. They are of the second quarter of the fourteenth century BC and were found in the palace of Akhenaten at el-Amarna in Upper Egypt. In several of them the king promises the pharaoh copper, and asks in return for gifts of silver and luxury goods, like a bedstead of ebony inlaid with gold and a gold chariot. References to *Alashiya* or *Asy* occur in other Near Eastern documents from Egypt, Syria and Anatolia. The earliest is of the eighteenth century and the latest of the twelfth century BC. From these we learn that *Alashiya* supplied copper to Syria and Anatolia in return for finished articles. The country was an island and, besides a king, it had its own fleet in the late thirteenth century BC. In the twelfth century BC it was overcome by the 'Sea Peoples', bands of adventurers roaming the Mediterranean. Earlier, in the fourteenth century, it was an ally of Egypt and an enemy of the Hittites, who were then struggling to gain control over Syria. Debate has raged over the location of *Alashiya* (or *Asy*) ever since it was first identified as Cyprus in 1895. Today many scholars would support such an identification, though some suggest it refers to a single site such as Enkomi rather than the whole island.

There are, however, major stumbling blocks, among them the language and script used by the king of *Alashiya* – on present evidence the Cypriot script at this time was Cypro-Minoan but, as it is undeciphered, the language is unknown.

Whatever the answer is to the *Alashiya* problem, recent work has thrown doubts on Cyprus' role in the copper trade in the Late Bronze Age. There are paradoxes in the evidence. At the time of the greatest activity on the part of the metalworkers in Minoan Crete and Mycenaean Greece in the sixteenth and fifteenth centuries BC contact with Cyprus was very limited whereas, when Mycenaean Greek pottery flooded the Cypriot market in the fourteenth and most of the thirteenth century, the Greek world was apparently suffering an acute metal shortage. This archaeological evidence, combined with results of scientific tests showing that certain items from Crete are not made of Cypriot copper, suggest that Cyprus was not the major supplier of copper to the west at this time. Nonetheless there is, as yet, little to contradict the view that Cypriot copper was exported to the Near East and Egypt. A shipwreck recently discovered off Kaş in southern Turkey contains a vast number of ingots of copper, as well as some of tin and glass, said to date from the fourteenth century BC. If the dating is correct and the copper ingots are of Cypriot copper, the island's role as an exporter to the east at this period would again be confirmed.

The products of Cypriot metalworkers in the Late Bronze Age were at first (until about 1450 BC) steeped in the old traditions. Little new influence from east or west is apparent in either the techniques or designs. Only from the area of the Bay of Morphou come a few bronze items of apparently Minoan (Cretan) origin. These were found along with vessels from Minoan Crete and Mycenaean Greece, which suggests, perhaps, some isolated connection between the Aegean and that part of Cyprus alone. In spite of industrial evidence from many of the settlement sites, there is little bronzework from securely dated contexts in Cyprus after around 1450 until late in the thirteenth century BC.

It was probably at about this time, towards the end of the Late Bronze Age, that the Cypriot industry was transformed under foreign influence. Many of the innovations had their origins in Mycenaean Greece but others came from Egypt or the Near East. Techniques previously very rare or completely unknown were practised, several of which are described in Chapter 4. These included elaborate work in sheet metal to form vessels, which now became much more common; casting in a two-piece mould to make tools with a central socket for the handle; lost-wax casting of statuettes and lead-filled weights in the form of animals or human heads, and hard soldering to join together parts of tripods and other vessel stands that had been made in separate pieces. These last, including some that were cast in one piece, are technical masterpieces produced in Cypriot workshops, mainly between the late thirteenth and mid-twelfth centuries BC. The decoration is partly in the *ajouré* (openwork) technique and the designs show a blend of Aegean and Near Eastern elements. They travelled westwards to Greece and the Aegean islands and even to

16 Cypriot bronze weight in the form of a bull, partially filled with lead. It weighs 87.12 grams and so conforms to the Mesopotamian standard. From the sanctuary of Apollo at Idalion, late 13th century BC. L 4.8 cm.

Italy, where they seem to have survived to be dedicated as heirlooms between the eleventh and seventh centuries BC.

The exact date of this revolution in the Cypriot bronze industry is difficult to determine but much of the evidence comes from hoards which were deposited in the twelfth century BC. Among these is the 'foundry hoard', which was found at Enkomi in 1897 probably in the north-western part of the site. Unfortunately no precise records were made at the time of its discovery and a complete inventory is lacking. Nonetheless, the hoard appears to be the contents of a smithy comprising the smith's own tools and new tools for carpentry and agricultural work. Other articles, like the weapons and vessel stands, were presumably for sale. Fragmentary vessels, stands, weapons and the waste left over from the casting process are all scrap metal, which must have been set aside for remelting. The ingots are unworked copper; the only complete example is shaped like an oxhide, and this is the form in which copper was transported, whether within the island or overseas.

Much bronzework has been found in early Iron Age Cyprus. Of Cypriot origin and manufacture are *fibulae* (brooches) with triangular bows strengthened with wire and beads and bowls whose handles are decorated with lotus flowers. Both these types spread eastwards and westwards from Cyprus. The *fibulae* reached Palestine, Greece, Sardinia and even Spain, where they were imitated locally, while the bowls travelled to the Near East, Greece and Italy. Phoenician immigrants were probably responsible for the lampstands and some of the metal bowls decorated with intricate scenes. The bronze harness and horse trappings and the vessels from the tombs of the aristocrats at Salamis were imported from or influenced by different parts of the Near East. Continued industrial activity is apparent from the discovery of copper workshops at Kition and

17 (*Right*) Bronze smithy tools from the Enkomi 'foundry hoard': a furnace spatula for managing red-hot charcoal, a charcoal shovel and a pair of tongs; 12th century BC. L (of shovel) 52.3 cm.

18 (*Below*) Bronze *fibula* (brooch). This typically Cypriot type of the early Iron Age spread eastwards, and westwards even to Spain, where local copies were made; c.7th century BC. L 18.5 cm.

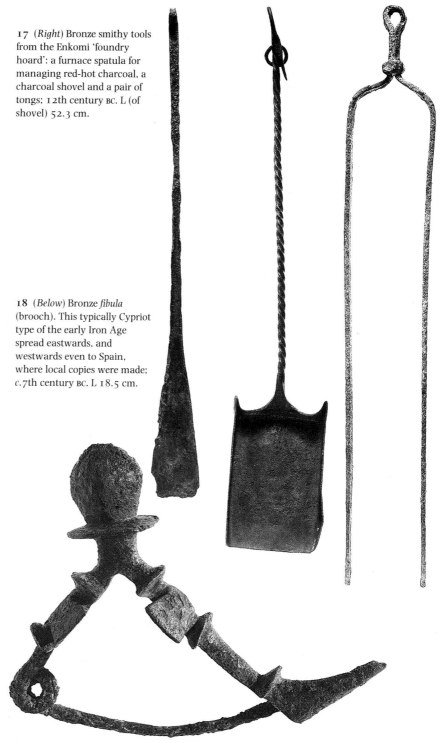

19

21

20 (*Below right*) Bronze head of a youth. It was probably cast abroad in southern Asia Minor but the modelling of the head may have been carried out elsewhere, perhaps in Cyprus. From Soloi, mid-2nd century AD. Ht 25.5 cm.

19 (*Below*) Bronze lampstand; the lamp rested on the ring between the 'arms' supported by the column decorated with lotus flowers. Such lampstands were probably made by Phoenician craftsmen resident in Cyprus; *c*. 8th century BC. Ht 26.4 cm.

Tamassos. The former were in use from about 650 to 450 BC and the latter from the seventh century BC into the Hellenistic period.

Copper was one of the principal attractions of Cyprus to the Ptolemies and the Romans. The Ptolemies themselves took over control of the mines, putting an official called an *antistrategos* ('lieutenant-general') in charge. Like almost all high officials, he would have been a non-Cypriot directly appointed by the king of Egypt. Large bronze statues were certainly cast hollow by the lost-wax process in Cyprus from about the first century BC. A bronze foundry of the late Hellenistic or early Roman period was found in Cyprus in the house of Dionysos at Paphos (the new town founded in the late fourth century BC). Cypriot bronzework of this period is for the most part indistinguishable from that produced elsewhere in the Mediterranean world. Among the artefacts were surgical instruments, toilet articles and statuettes. Even the bronze portraits so far discovered on the island were apparently cast abroad, probably in southern Asia Minor. However, the modelling of the face of a head from Soloi of the mid-second century AD may have been carried out in Cyprus. Like the Ptolemies, the Romans obtained for themselves the direct benefit from the copper mines. Their working was farmed out to contractors under the central control of a Roman procurator. (In 12 BC half the production of the Soloi mines was leased to Herod of Judaea.) Nonetheless, the island must have profited from the presence of such a large-scale industrial enterprise.

4 Trade and manufacture

Her geographical position alone ensured Cyprus' role as a major trading post in antiquity. Tucked in the eastern corner of the Mediterranean, she lies at the crossroads of seaborne trade between the ancient civilisations of Anatolia to the north, Egypt to the south, Greece and Rome to the west and Mesopotamia and Persia to the east. Then, as now, her strategic importance did not go unnoticed. She was subjected to foreign rule, fought over and used as a battleground. At different times she was a major supplier to the ancient world of copper, corn and timber for ship-building. In her own right she was a manufacturing centre and, using resources of her own as well as imported materials, she produced highly individual works of art and various artefacts. We are fortunate that many pottery vessels have survived from ancient Cyprus. Many of these vases were made locally and illustrate the ingenuity of Cypriot potters throughout antiquity. Others were imported from different parts of the Mediterranean world. These in particular help to provide a picture of the island's trading contacts and their consequences.

Overseas trade was not properly established for a long time after the arrival of the earliest settlers, some time before 7000 BC, probably from the nearby Syrian coast. It is likely, therefore, that these settlers brought with them the more exotic materials, like obsidian (originally from south–central Anatolia), cornelian and mother-of-pearl, that have been found at their settlement sites. They did not make pottery, but used andesite, a grey–green

21 Divers excavating the stern of a Greek merchant ship which sank off the coast at Kyrenia at the end of the 4th century BC. The cargo included amphorae from Rhodes containing wine, and others from Samos filled with oil, millstones (for ballast) from the island of Nisyros and 10,000 almonds which had probably just been collected from Cyprus.

22 Three vessels of Red Polished ware with incised decoration: **a)** a jug with a double cut-away beaked spout from Alambra; **b)** a deep tulip-shaped bowl with lug handles from Vounous; **c)** a round-mouthed jug. The deep bowl is two-coloured, being black on the rim and the interior, and the incisions of the beaked jug are filled with white paint. Early and Middle Bronze Age, 2300–1800 BC. Ht (of beaked jug) 29.8 cm.

stone obtainable from the river-beds, for their vases and figurines. Sickle blades and arrow-heads of flint were made to support their farming economy.

In the later Neolithic period (4600/4500–4000/3900 BC) handmade pottery was produced in Cyprus. In the north designs were painted in red on a white ground, sometimes using a brush with multiple heads; in the south patterns were made by 'combing' the slip (a specially prepared clay solution used for coating vessels) with a tool with multiple teeth.

The hallmarks of the Chalcolithic period (3900–2500 BC) – the advent of metal, the

cruciform figurines and the new burial customs – are all discussed elsewhere. Red-on-White painted pottery, now produced in the south as well as the north, continued the earlier tradition, but towards the end of the period some monochrome vessels were made. Their final colour depended on the firing conditions in a manner foreshadowing practices of the Bronze Age.

There are unmistakable south Anatolian traits in the Cypriot products of the succeeding era, which ushered in the Bronze Age, notably in the pottery and metal forms. Red Polished became the dominant pottery ware lasting into the Middle Bronze Age. The vessels were still handmade and covered by a slip, which was burnished and then often decorated with patterns incised with a sharp-edged cutting edge before being fired. The final colour of the slip, and so the appearance of the vessel, depended on the amount of iron oxide in the solution (more was needed for it to become red, less for black), and the conditions and temperature of firing. By exercising tight control over the cooling as well as the firing conditions potters were able to produce vessels that were either mottled or two-coloured. The latter were often mainly red on the outside but black on the exterior of the rim and the inside. Favourite shapes were shallow bowls and round-bottomed jugs, either with beaked 'cut-away' spouts or tall necks with round flaring mouths. More elaborate items produced in this fabric included human and animal figurines and deep bowls with various attachments.

Some painted pottery was produced in the Early Bronze Age but the start of the Middle Bronze Age, around 1900 BC, is marked by the beginning of a new tradition of painted wares. The handmade vessels were carefully burnished. The decoration of linear patterns in reddish brown or dark brown on a light ground gave the ware its name, White Painted. Analysis of the decoration has made it possible to distinguish certain regional styles. In the east of the island, for example, straight or wavy lines set vertically or at an angle so as to cross each other were popular, while in the north the pattern structure was more formal. Brushes with multiple heads were used more frequently in eastern Cyprus, notably on the Karpas Peninsula, which was the home of another painted ware, Red-on-Black (or Red-on-Red); the designs were painted in red on a black (or red) ground. In the south and extreme west of the island, monochrome vases continued to be made although without incised decoration.

It was during the Early and Middle Bronze

23 a) A dish with a wishbone handle and b) a juglet which, if turned upside down, resembles an opium poppy. Of Base Ring ware (the juglet decorated with white painted lines), such vessels were widely exported. The dish from Phoenikiais or Alambra was made between 1550 and 1450 BC, and the juglet (also from Cyprus) is of 1650–1500 BC. Ht (of juglet) 14.6 cm.

24 Two vessels of White Slip ware: a) a 'milk bowl' (with a true wishbone handle); b) a tankard. The latter is decorated with fine lines in two colours, not a very common technique for this ware, which was widely exported, particularly the 'milk bowls'. Both pieces were found in Cyprus, the tankard at Maroni, and were made between 1650 and 1450 BC. Ht (of tankard) 20.2 cm.

Age that Cyprus was beginning to emerge from her isolation. First contacts were made with Crete, while commercial relations were established with the Near East (Syria and Palestine), Egypt and, towards the end of the period, southern Anatolia.

In the early stages of the Late Bronze Age (c. 1650–1450 BC), Cypriot civilisation was for the most part deeply rooted in its past, most apparent from the bronzework and other smaller artefacts. Base Ring and White Slip became the dominant wares of fine pottery until about 1200 BC. Significantly both were handmade in the old tradition. Base Ring takes its name from the ring-shaped bases applied to nearly every vessel in the group. The vases have unusually thin walls, normally covered by a highly polished brown slip. The decoration, if any, consists of relief bands and white painted lines. The most common shapes are jugs with tall necks and flaring mouths, little [23] jugs (or juglets) and bowls with 'wishbone' handles. The juglets may have been inspired by an inverted poppy head and used as containers for opium (see p.8). It is likely too that the bodies were made in moulds. Whatever the truth of the opium hypothesis, the juglets and also the dishes with wishbone handles were exported to Egypt, Syria and Palestine. The thick white slip which covers [24] the vessels of White Slip ware would have been very pure. This was painted with linear patterns in orange, brown or black, or occasionally in two colours. Round-bottomed bowls with wishbone handles, known as 'milk bowls', were widely exported to the east but presumably for their aesthetic value rather than their contents, since they could not be sealed.

Early in the Late Bronze Age some pottery was imported from Egypt and Palestine. The Egyptian vases inspired local imitations. From around 1600 BC, for no more than about fifty [9] years, pottery of a distinctive Palestinian type was produced in eastern Cyprus. The vases were thrown on a fast wheel and decorated in red and black (the Bichrome technique) with geometric and floral patterns and figured scenes. These workshops were comparatively short-lived, and had no influence on the contemporary handmade tradition. The same is true of slightly later (1550–1250 BC) wheel-made pottery, which is covered by a glossy red slip. This ware originated in southern Anatolia, but was also produced in Syria and Palestine, which would have supplied the Cyprus market if the vases found there were not made locally.

The pottery production, therefore, illustrates Cyprus' close relations with the Near East and Egypt from early in the Late Bronze Age. In the fourteenth and thirteenth centuries BC urban centres including Enkomi, Kition, Hala Sultan Tekké, Maroni and Old Paphos (several of them established shortly before 1600 BC) enjoyed great prosperity. Materials like gold, ivory and faience, and some finished articles were imported. Cypriot workshops made jewellery, sealstones and artefacts of glass, faience and ivory. Their products show an amalgam of local and foreign influences and are of a high technical quality. Some contacts were established with Italy, Sicily and Sardinia. Cypriots were actually living at Ugarit on the Syrian coast. From there in the thirteenth century BC came the original inspiration for the construction of buildings with fine ashlar blocks, a tradition which continued in Cyprus in the twelfth century BC and in the Iron Age.

Also during the fourteenth and most of the thirteenth centuries a great quantity of pottery was imported by Cyprus from Mycenaean Greece. These Mycenaean vessels are all wheel-made, usually of fine clay covered by a creamy-buff slip on which the designs were painted in glossy brown (it sometimes turned to red on firing). Particularly popular in Cyprus were large vessels such as amphorae (storage jars) and kraters (bowls for mixing

25 (*Above*) Faience vessel in the form of a closed lotus flower decorated with the Egyptian god of infinity Ḥeḥ holding lotus flowers. Probably made in Egypt, c.1400–1200 BC. From Enkomi. Ht 22.3 cm.

27 (*Right*) Ivory gaming box decorated with hunting scenes and animals. The squares on the top of the box are arranged for the Egyptian game of *Tjau*; underneath is a drawer for the gaming pieces. The bottom of the box was marked out for the game of *Senet*. Found at Enkomi and made in the 12th century BC. It was probably carved in Cyprus from ivory imported from Syria or Egypt. L 29.1 cm.

wine and water) decorated with processions of chariots, bulls and birds. It is not clear what Cyprus sent to Greece in return for all this pottery. Very few of her own contemporary vases or other artefacts have been found in the Greek world, and, as we have already seen, it is unlikely that copper was supplied to the west at this time. Exports might have included perishables like grain, textiles or timber. It is likely that trade was in the hands of independent entrepreneurs who plied the routes, setting up and putting down goods wherever profit was to be made. In that way they could dispense with the need to balance the books precisely between different countries.

Towards the end of the thirteenth century BC the supply of Mycenaean pottery dwindled. In response to this, Cypriot potters started to make their own imitations and so, at last, generally adopted the fast wheel. For a short time, until about 1200 BC, some vases, usually bell-shaped kraters bore pictorial decoration, often of bulls or goats executed in a 'rude' (or 'pastoral') style. Longer-lasting and still produced in the twelfth century BC were shallow

dishes (and a few other shapes) with linear designs.

Cyprus was caught up in the tribulations that affected the whole Mediterranean world at this time. Her own twelfth-century civilisation enjoyed a certain amount of prosperity. Strong influence from Mycenaean Greece and Crete is apparent, particularly on the pottery, bronzework and sealstones, but the jewellery, faience and ivory work owe much to the Near East. The whole is, as before, an amalgam of Cypriot, Aegean and Eastern elements. Relations with the far west were intensified and some Cypriot bronzeworkers went abroad to settle and work in Sicily and Sardinia.

Around 1125 BC a new pottery ware, Proto-White Painted, was first made by Cypriot potters. Since its shapes and ornaments are mostly of Greek origin and it is the forerunner of the principal Iron Age fabric, it may speak for the arrival of Greeks already in the twelfth century BC. Specifically Cretan are certain forms, including the straight-sided box (pyxis), kalathos (basket-like vase) and a particular type of flask shaped like a bird. Influence from Syria and Palestine accounts for certain

26 Mycenaean vessel (amphoroid krater) decorated with a procession of chariots. Many vessels decorated in this pictorial style have been found in Cyprus and they were perhaps made in Mycenaean Greece particularly for export. From near Maroni, 14th century BC. Ht 41.9 cm.

29 A jug and a perfume flask of Black-on-Red ware, both from Amathus and made in Cyprus. The jug with its flat bottom is a Phoenician shape, while the perfume flask is an example of the type exported to some Greek islands and closely imitated in Crete. The ridge for the handle was used by Cypriot potters at the beginning of the Iron Age for jugs with barrel-shaped bodies; 800–750 BC. Ht (of flask) 13.4 cm.

28 Flask in the form of bird of White Painted ware. The bird shape for flasks was introduced to Cyprus from Crete and appears in the Cypriot pottery repertoire from around 1125 BC. This example was made between about 1050 and 1000 BC. L 22 cm.

shapes and motifs. Sometimes designs were painted in two colours, recalling the technique of some White Slip vessels.

Although groups of settlers from the Greek world may have arrived intermittently in Cyprus during the twelfth century BC, the most massive migrations probably happened around 1100 BC. It is in cemeteries of the eleventh century BC that tombs of the Mycenaean Greek type occur alongside the traditional Cypriot graves (p.53) and only then did the Cypro-Minoan script finally die out. Ironworking had been practised in Cyprus from around 1150 BC, and it was probably from Cyprus that the new technology was introduced to Greece in the early eleventh century. This also points to close contacts between the two areas at the time. The jewellery, principally of eastern types, and the metalwork continuing the Aegean tradition, found with pottery in the first half of the eleventh century, are evidence of some prosperity.

Even during the first two hundred years of the Iron Age (1050–850 BC), normally described as a 'Dark Age', some contacts were maintained with both east and west. The most common fine pottery is White Painted, with the ornaments in black or brown on a buff or greenish-white slip. This had its origins in the fabric produced at the very end of the Late Bronze Age. New influence from Syria and Palestine accounts for the re-appearance of Bichrome Ware which has in addition broad areas painted in matt red. A new shape at this period is a barrel-shaped jug with a ridge opposite the handle, inspired by a type of bottle made earlier in Syria and Palestine. Some of the decorative motifs, like the schematic birds, have their origin in Late Bronze Age Crete, but others, like wild goats, the 'tree of life' and circle patterns, are of eastern inspiration.

The arrival of the Phoenician settlers in Cyprus, at least at Kition in the mid-ninth century BC, prompted a revival in Cypriot culture. Typical Phoenician pottery, both Red Slip (the vases are covered by a red coating) and Black-on-Red (with black ornaments on the red ground) had been imported earlier, but it was henceforth locally made as well. The shapes in the local repertoire included some of Phoenician origin, like the deep bowls with linear decoration and flat-bottomed juglets with bands around the belly and concentric circles on the shoulders. Others imitated those in the contemporary White Painted and Bichrome fabrics, which in turn were also made in the 'Phoenician' shapes. Overall the standard of Cypriot potting improved greatly. Ornaments were more carefully drawn, and further attempts were made at a purely pictorial style.

Greek pottery from Athens and Euboea had started arriving in Cyprus around 950 BC. By the late tenth century Cypriot exports had reached Euboea, where it seems likely that the local bronze industry was revived under Cypriot tuition. Following the arrival of the Phoenicians, the volume of imported Greek pottery increased. In the eighth century some may have been brought by Euboeans on their way to the Syrian coast, since at that time Cyprus and Euboea were apparently sharing the trade with Al Mina. Copies of Euboean vases were also made locally by Cypriot potters. Crete received a number of eastern and eastern-inspired goods between the tenth and eighth centuries, all of which probably travelled by way of Cyprus. Cyprus' own pottery reached Crete from the late ninth century. Crete was in fact one of the three islands, the others being Rhodes and Cos, that received a steady supply of Cypriot pottery starting soon after the arrival of the Phoenicians at Kition. Many of these exports were slow-pouring Black-on-Red perfume jugs. They were imitated locally in the eighth century BC, perhaps to contain perfume produced in small factories set up and staffed by Phoenicians from Cyprus.

The Archaic period had begun about 750 BC and this (lasting until 475 BC) was another era of great prosperity for Cyprus, notwithstanding her domination by three foreign powers (Assyria *c*.709–669 BC, Egypt *c*.570/60–545 and then Persia from *c*.545 BC). The island had wide-ranging commercial contacts and played an increasingly important role in international trade. A number of artefacts of Near Eastern origin, imported or imitated by the Cypriots, reached not only the Greek world but also Phoenician centres in the western Mediterranean. Direct contacts were maintained with Syria and Phoenicia, while Phoenician immigrants in Cyprus were probably responsible for the production of some fine metalwork. Within the Greek world Cyprus' relations were principally with the East Greek cities established on the west coast of Asia Minor and the neighbouring islands. East Greek pottery was imported and some attempts were made to imitate it locally. Cypriot goods were exported, notably to Samos, Rhodes and Euboea. Closer contacts were established with Egypt during the period of her rule, when Cypriot statuettes were exported to Naucratis, the Greek trading post in the Egyptian Delta, where they inspired local copies. In Cyprus itself signs of Egyptian influence at this time include the production of strongly Egyptianising bronze statuettes, a painted burial chamber at Salamis and a dedication to the goddess Isis. Around 700 BC a Cypriot dedication was made at the 'international' shrine at Delphi, the first evidence of an association that was to last into the second century AD.

The inclusion of Cyprus in the Persian Empire around 545 BC brought her into closer contact with the East Greek cities of Asia Minor, which had suffered the same fate. Athens had, however, now won all the foreign markets for pottery and so the Greek pottery in Cyprus, as elsewhere, is mainly Attic (Athenian). This resulted in some imitation by

Cypriot potters and also in some Attic vases being made in Cypriot shapes, apparently specifically aimed at the Cypriot market.

The political organisation of the island into autonomous city–kingdoms led to the development of regional styles, stimulated to some extent by the swift succession of foreign overlords. Regionalism is particularly apparent in the pottery, although the wares remained the same as in the previous period and the shapes were generally developed from those of their precursors. The attractive pictorial style became characteristic of the south and east. A wide variety of scenes were depicted, drawing their inspiration mainly from Syrian and Phoenician textiles and minor art, like ivory carvings, decorated metalwork and sealstones. In the north and west potters concentrated on producing intricate shapes with elaborate circle patterns. The pottery of Amathus has close-packed decoration.

The Classical period (about 475–325 BC) found Cyprus poised between Greece and Persia. Persia increased her control after the failure of the Ionian Revolt, an attempt by the East Greek cities of Asia Minor to free themselves from Persian rule, in which the Cypriot cities participated. Athens made some attempts to liberate the island in the first half of the fifth century BC (see p.16). Attic pottery continued to dominate the market and inspiration from Classical Greece is apparent in several media. Phoenician influence spread within the island. Lapithos and Marion had Phoenician kings in the fifth century; Kition acquired the kingdom of Idalion around 450 BC (and a century later the kingdom of Tamassos). Soon after the mid-fifth century BC the Phoenicians had even established a dynasty at Salamis, a traditionally Greek city. However, for the forty years after his seizure of the throne at Salamis in about 411 BC the Greek Cypriot Evagoras I dominated Cypriot politics and openly welcomed Greek imports and immigrants. A colony of Salaminians was established in Athens and in the late fourth century the Kitians established a shrine in the Athenian port of Piraeus.

Greek influence therefore permeated certain Cypriot products of the fifth and fourth centuries BC, although eastern influence is still apparent and the Cypriot character survived. In pottery the same fabrics were employed. Bichrome Red, which adds decoration in white to the traditional Black-on-Red, had been known occasionally earlier but now became more popular. The vessels were generally taller and slimmer. A few new types were introduced, among them a jug with a *kore* (Greek maiden) on the neck holding a smaller jug, which acts as a spout. Greek ornaments were copied. A few attempts were made to imitate the Greek red-figure technique with the decoration reserved (i.e., in the colour of the clay) against a dark background and with the details painted. Contacts with Syria and Phoenicia were maintained. Cypriot sculpture was exported, while imports from Phoenicia included mummy-shaped sarcophagi (p.54), which were imitated by the Phoenicians at Kition. Phoenician building techniques were sometimes employed. Cyprus obviously had relations with the ruling power, though Persian influence on her civilisation is restricted to the plans of certain buildings (or 'palaces') and a few shapes and ornaments mostly for items of precious metal.

Although Alexander the Great released the Cypriot kingdoms from Persian control in 333 BC, he also took away some of their autonomy, and when the island was annexed by Ptolemy I of Egypt in 294 BC they finally ceased to exist.

Cyprus became part of the large Hellenistic state of Egypt. As such she became artistically orientated to the Hellenistic world and her own products in general conform to the cosmopolitan styles of the period. As she was now part of the Greek world, her athletes took part in the Panathenaic and Olympic games and sculptors from Salamis worked at Delphi and at Lindos in Rhodes. She maintained particularly close ties with Egypt, shown by sculpture in the Ptolemaic style as well as burial customs and architectural features that reflect fashions in the newly founded Egyptian city of Alexandria. Fine glasses and pottery were imported from Syria and Asia Minor, but Cyprus' own workshops were very active. Glassmaking was revived, with the manufacture of little amphorae with s-shaped handles, formed of coloured glass around a removable core, and small pendants in the form of female heads made by a similar technique. The earlier White Painted and Plain White fabrics survived, but Cypriot workshops also made versions of the common Greek black glaze (vases covered by a glossy black slip), including some with moulded, impressed or white painted decoration, and the red slip wares of Asia Minor. Mould-made lamps were produced in local workshops, but the jewellery, terracotta figurines, bronzework and other small artefacts conform to the types found throughout the Hellenistic world.

Under Roman rule Cyprus came fully under the influence of the civilisation of the Empire, which especially in the east was rooted in Hellenistic traditions. Consequently the language and culture of the island remained basically Greek. The predominant fine pottery of the earlier Roman period was a fabric covered by a glossy red slip. It was locally produced, the shapes mainly copying the vases of Syria and southern Asia Minor. Dishes, bowls and jugs found a ready market in Cyprus. Many vessels had a low foot, and jugs

32 Pottery and glass of the Hellenistic period found in Cyprus and dating from the 3rd to the 1st century BC; **a**) a core-formed glass scent bottle with s-shaped handles, made in Cyprus; **b**) a skyphos (cup) with white painted decoration, perhaps made in Cyprus; **c**) a Grey ware bowl (drinking cup), perhaps made in Asia Minor; **d**) a clay lamp, made in Cyprus; **e**) a *lagynos* (wine-jug) decorated with fishes and possibly made in Cyprus. Ht (of *lagynos*) 17.8 cm.

often had angled handles. This local Red Slip ware became particularly widespread within Cyprus from the first century AD. It was widely exported in the east in the second century, and the occasional piece reached the west. Potters at New Paphos apparently had direct links with the west; many vessels of the first and second century AD imported from Campania in southern Italy have been found in the house of Dionysos. Vases with a lead glaze were imported from Tarsus in southern Asia Minor, and a few vessels came from Egypt. The glass industry throughout the Roman world was transformed by the invention of glass-blowing in the mid-first century BC. Previously a luxury product, glass now became much more widely available. Workshops producing the common blown glasses were established in Cyprus, as they were elsewhere in the Roman Empire. Favourite shapes of the Cypriot glass-blowers

were jars, beakers and flasks for oil or perfume. Some of the jars had the lid decorated with a design painted on the inside so as to be viewed through the glass. The paint itself was not fired on and so flakes away very easily. Cypriot glassware was exported to the Black Sea, the Greek world and northern Italy, but the more elaborate vessels were still imported, principally from Syrian glasshouses. Skilled craftsmen working in Cyprus were responsible for a fine series of mosaics. Sculptors, bronzeworkers and jewellers remained active, though specifically Cypriot products are often difficult to identify. Cyprus had become an integral part of the Roman east with its basically Greek language and culture which were to have a profound influence on her later history.

33 Pottery and glass of the Roman period found in Cyprus and most probably made there: a) a clay lamp; b) a Red Slip ware wine-jug; c) a blown-glass bottle for oil or perfume; d) a blown-glass bowl with painted lid; e) a Red Slip ware bowl; f) a White ware wine-jug with decoration resembling that of glasses with wheel-cut patterns; g) a blown-glass lid with a figure of Eros painted on the inside; h) a clay lamp signed on the bottom by a Cypriot lamp-maker; i) a Red Slip ware wine-jug. Most of these pieces date between the 1st and 2nd centuries AD, although the signed lamp is of the 3rd-4th century. Ht (of i) 22.8 cm.

33b

4

5 The human form in Cypriot art

The human form appeared in the art of the earliest inhabitants of Cyprus and remained a dominant theme throughout antiquity. With a few exceptions the figures of the Neolithic period were quite small, no more than 19cm in height, and made of stone; they are rather elementary representations of the human form, with the arms and legs reduced to mere stumps. The latest examples of this type (including one from Lemba which is 36cm tall) are contemporary with another variety typical of the succeeding Chalcolithic era (4000/3900–2500 BC). Shaped like a cross, almost invariably made of soft-stone (bluish-green picrolite or serpentine), this type has now been shown to have developed within Cyprus from the stump-like form. The cruciform category includes some figures of terracotta. An interesting repertoire in that material shows the ingenuity of the Chalcolithic artists.

Bronze Age representations differ from their predecessors in both style and the preferred material. In the Early and Middle phases (2300–1650 BC) plank-shaped figurines of terracotta predominate. Made in fabrics akin to those of the contemporary pottery, Red Polished and White Painted, they bear incised or painted decoration. The most typical have a rectangular body on which is placed a narrower and smaller rectangle for the head and neck. Some pieces have two heads. Red Polished examples have incised patterns indicating headbands, necklaces, belts and facial features. Some of either fabric have modelled noses or small ears and perhaps crudely formed breasts; they may cradle a child in their arms. The great majority of these are quite small, between about 18 and 26cm in height, which emphasises how exceptionally large the White Painted example illustrated here must have been, since the surviving head and neck already measure 17cm. This is perhaps an example of another plank-shaped type, which has the head and body of roughly the same

width, so that there are no real shoulders. Others are in the form of 'combs' or 'brushes': they have long thin necks and square bodies, often decorated on the lower half with vertical incised lines. Since some Chalcolithic examples of this type made of picrolite are now known, it may be that the plank-shaped type, like the cruciform variety, developed in Cyprus itself. It cannot, however, be denied that such figurines (of terracotta) were being produced in southern Anatolia at the time and this was perhaps one of the new and foreign ideas from that region that helped to usher in the Bronze Age to Cyprus.

Early and Middle Bronze Age potters seldom included representations of human beings in the incised or painted decoration on their vases, but were nonetheless happy to model them in clay: figures sit on the edge of bowls,

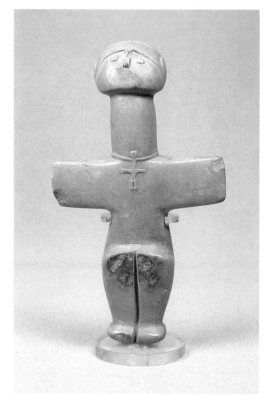

34 Picrolite (soft-stone) figurine shaped like a cross and wearing a necklace with a pendant of similar form. From Yialia. 3500–2500 BC. Ht 15.3 cm.

grow out of them or are formed out of the pot itself. They are simply made, with solid bodies and schematic heads and arms; terracotta models show similar figures taking part in various activities. There are scarcely any human figures in stone of this period and indeed only a very few among all the terracotta examples are depicted fully in the round.

At the end of the Middle Bronze Age, though continuing to work in clay, artists made radical changes in the way they represented human figures. They are now obviously female, having a curving rather than straight outline, with wide hips and an incised pubic triangle. They are usually portrayed standing with their hands held just below their breasts. This type of figurine originated in the east in the third millennium BC and reached Cyprus by way of Syria. Closest to their Syrian

36 (*Above*) Vessels of White Painted ware of the Middle and beginning of the Late Bronze Age, late 18th–16th century BC: a bottle with human figure growing out of it, probably from Idalion; a bottle in quasi-human form; a boat with a human figure sitting on its edge; a jug with a human figure on the shoulder. Ht (of jug) 21 cm.

35 (*Far left*) Plank-shaped figure of White Painted ware; the upper part of an exceptionally large example; 1725–1625 BC. Ht 17 cm.

37 (*Left*) Two female figurines of terracotta with their hands below their breasts. One wears a flat cap squashing down the ears; the ears of the other are large and pierced and adorned with earrings. Both from Enkomi, *c*.1450–1200 BC. Ht (of example with cap) 21.3 cm.

prototypes are those with large flanged ears, sometimes adorned with earrings. A second variety has a flattened head with the ears apparently squashed down by a hat, perhaps a sign of Mycenaean Greek influence.

While the prehistoric representations of the human form can be classified into broad groups in a roughly chronological succession, Iron Age portrayals are more diverse. The greatest innovation was the production of large-scale (life-size or even larger) statues in stone, terracotta and, more rarely, bronze. This happened in Cyprus around the middle of the seventh century BC, when the island was enjoying a period of independence from foreign rule. Smaller (less than life-size) statuettes were produced in similar styles in the same materials. Vast numbers of yet smaller figures of terracotta in various techniques and types were also made. Many of these figures, both large and small, were dedicated in sanctuaries, and it seems that the major shrines had their own workshops ready to supply visiting pilgrims. In the Hellenistic and more particularly the Roman period statues of rulers and gods were set up in public places and adorned municipal buildings. Painted and model representations decorate pottery vessels, and others are included in the designs on sealstones and on metal vessels and utensils.

The two-dimensional representations of the earlier Iron Age generally portray eastern figures. This is hardly surprising, since the painted vases were inspired by Syrian and Phoenician textiles and minor art, such as ivories, metalwork and seals. In addition, a number of the metal bowls and other artefacts were most probably made by Phoenician craftsmen resident in Cyprus. The women usually have their hair in a plain mass, often combed into a bun at the nape of the neck and sometimes with a curling lock falling forward by the ear. They wear long plain robes, often of patterned material. The men, if not in Egyptian costume of crown and kilt, are usually dressed and equipped as warriors with conical helmets and large round shields.

Until about 475 BC small terracotta figurines often had trumpet-shaped or conical bodies. The solid pieces were handmade, but some of the hollow ones were formed on a wheel. Less common are examples with bell-shaped wheel-made bodies, sometimes with detachable legs. The arms were simply modelled and might be upraised, hold an object close to the body or, for the women, hold the breasts. At first all heads were handmade. They were peg-like, with prominent noses and with the top often formed into a hat, a pointed 'bonnet' (or helmet) for the men and a rectangular crown (*polos*) for the women. In the early

38 Interior of a bowl of Bichrome ware decorated with pairs of women; they wear long robes, with their hair falling down to the nape of the neck, and stand on either side of 'lotus flower' trees, sniffing flowers. From Achna, 6th century BC. D 34.3 cm.

39 (*Right*) Painted terracotta head from a statue of a bearded worshipper in the earliest style of Iron Age Cypriot sculpture. From the sanctuary of Apollo at Phrangissa, Tamassos, 650–600 BC. Ht 36 cm.

40 (*Below*) Limestone head from a statue of a bearded worshipper with his hair arranged in an Egyptian-style *klaft* (wig) plaited with strings. From the sanctuary of Apollo at Idalion, *c.*550 BC. Ht 41 cm.

eighth century BC the use of moulds for terracottas was learnt by the Cypriots from Syria, and Cyprus in turn may have played a role in introducing this technique into Greece shortly afterwards. Thereafter, either the head alone or the whole figure might be made in a mould, and this heralds a notable change in style. The women now have more delicate features, often with wig-like hair. If the body too is moulded, the back is flat and the costume either a transparent tunic or a robe of thicker material with a sash, beneath a cloak pulled up over the head. The men too become more lifelike, and wear a wide variety of caps and helmets. Their normal dress is a long plain robe and a mantle.

58a

Cypriot sculptors in the Iron Age worked either in terracotta or locally available stone of different varieties, all commonly called 'limestone'. The large terracotta statues were hand-made in separate pieces and then joined together. The stone was relatively soft, lending itself to engraved and painted decoration

41 Terracotta figure of a female harp-player; she is bedecked with jewellery and her hair is arranged in spiral curls. From the sanctuary of Apollo at Idalion, early 6th century BC. Ht 30.7 cm.

42 (*Right*) Limestone statue of a male worshipper carrying a bird as an offering in his left hand and incense in a box in his right. In Greek fashion, his hair is short, secured by a laurel wreath, and he stands with his left leg advanced. He is dressed in Greek costume, a *chiton* (short-sleeved tunic) partly covered by a *himation* (cloak). From the sanctuary of Apollo at Idalion, c.475–450 BC. Ht 98 cm.

43 (*Left*) Limestone head from a statue of a worshipper made by a sculptor, who copied closely work of his famous Greek (Athenian) contemporaries like Pheidias and Polycleitus. From the sanctuary of Apollo at Idalion, 450–400 BC. Ht 18 cm.

rather than sharply carved detail. A particular characteristic of Cypriot limestone sculpture which survived into the Hellenistic period was that the backs of the statues were generally ignored, being left completely or virtually flat with no attempt to show details of the anatomy. Throughout antiquity marble was imported, at first in the fifth century BC from Greece, later also from Asia Minor (modern Turkey). A few finished statues of marble had reached Cyprus from Greece as early as the sixth century BC.

The earliest style of Iron Age Cypriot sculpture was essentially a local creation, although it shows some eastern influence. The faces are triangular or oval, the expressions severe and the eyes large and protruding, usually with 'feathered' eyebrows (they are decorated with 39 hatched lines). The men sport beards, which may be square like those of their earlier Assyrian rulers, and wear helmets. The women are bedecked with jewellery and their headdress is a turban or low crown. The usual dress for men and women, similar to that worn by the moulded terracottas, is an ankle-length 58b robe, partly covered by a cloak for the men. Both men and women stand with their feet together; the left arm is usually by the side and the right bent across the body, the women's holding an offering and the men's tucked in a fold of the cloak. By the early sixth century BC Cyprus came into contact with other Mediterranean powers. This led to the development of a new style which reflects influence from Egypt and the Greek east (the Greek cities on the coast of Asia Minor and the neighbouring islands), as well as the Near East. The hair is now usually arranged in an Egyptian-type *klaft* (wig), and in East Greek style the features 40 are softer, with a hint of a smile on the lips. The men continue to sport long beards, which are sometimes square as before, and they may wear a variety of helmets, mostly of Near Eastern types. Besides the eastern long robe

and mantle, a loin-cloth, perhaps of Greek origin, and a headband or an Egyptian-type kilt and crown may be worn. The women's costume and headdress are virtually unchan- 58c ged, and they continue to be bedecked with jewellery. Some have the Egyptian *klaft*, often covered by a veil, but for others the hair is 41 arranged in elaborate spiral curls familiar from Syrian and Phoenician ivory work.

About 545 BC Cyprus suffered the same fate as the East Greek cities of being absorbed into the Persian Empire, which from 539 BC also included Syria and Phoenicia. Freedom of movement within the Empire intensified contact between the areas. Cypriot sculptors became more dependent on East Greek models and influenced by Phoenician taste. Figures of men now normally wear a linen *chiton* (tunic) 42 and a woollen *himation* (cloak), the typical dress of the East Greek school, and stand with one foot advanced, like their models. Only occasionally are they naked in the mainland Greek tradition, although this form was occasionally adopted by Cypriot sculptors in the early sixth century BC. Some are clean-shaven, but others retain their beards, which are now artificially curled like those of their earlier Assyrian rulers. Similar curls appear on the back of the neck of some of those with long hair, who may keep their oriental helmets or Egyptian crowns, but others adopt the Greek short hairstyle, with curls over the forehead secured by a wreath. Stimulated in part by the resident Phoenician population, some sculptures wear Egyptian crowns and kilts reflecting the Phoenician fashion for Egyptianising statues. All now have softer, more rounded features and a distinct smile. The women have similar features and some continue to wear the traditional dress, but there are also some faithful copies of Greek *korai* (maidens), with their drapery falling in elaborate folds and long hair arranged in decorative patterns. The Cypriot versions keep their rich jewellery.

From 475 to 325 BC the political situation brought Cyprus into closer contact with mainland Greece. For representations of the human form this led to increasing Cypriot dependence on Greek models. There remain, however, some distinctly Cypriot limestone statues and statuettes. They continue the tradition established at the end of the sixth century: the men wear Greek costume and may have beards, perhaps artificially curled, and short hair curled over the forehead and secured by a wreath. Slowly this style stagnated and the later examples are very poorly carved. Alongside these are pieces that reflect the Classical style that had been developed in mainland Greece. They were perhaps partly inspired by imported works, like the bronze head from Tamassos, known as the 'Chatsworth Apollo' after its previous home. Nearly all small terracotta figurines were now made in moulds and some of the moulds themselves may have been imported from Greece. Greek dress is the norm, as are classical features. Maidens of a Greek type sit on the shoulders of vessels, pouring from a small jug. A series of horsemen is more readily identifiable as Cypriot. These keep their prominent noses and varied headdresses.

Cypriot sculptures of the Hellenistic and Roman periods in general reflect the styles which were fairly universal throughout the Greek-dominated eastern Mediterranean. Until the first century BC the Cypriot characteristics survived to some extent, since the principal medium remained the local 'limestone', and many of the statues continued to be dedicated in sanctuaries rather acting as memorials or decorating public buildings, as was the case elsewhere. Following the canon ascribed by the Roman author Pliny in the first century AD to the Greek sculptor Lysippos of Sikyon (active c.370/60–305 BC), the heads were smaller and the bodies more slender and tightly knit, so that the statues appeared taller.

45 Marble portrait head from a statue of a woman. Found in the gymnasium at Salamis, 2nd century AD. Ht 23 cm.

Portraits became more fashionable and many representations of worshippers appear to have their facial features based on those of their Ptolemaic rulers. Heads are normally fairly round and fleshy. Many men have their hair short and bound by a wreath, but some wear it long, arranged in corkscrew curls. The women's longer hair is often put up into a bun at the back, and a modified version of the *chiton*, now girded just below the breasts, became a favourite dress. The men's tunic is often only knee-length, while the cloak may be wrapped around the waist and then drawn up over the shoulder and partly across the body. Oriental figures wear Persian peaked caps made of soft material. Virtually all terracotta figurines were cast in moulds. Some, following the tradition of Alexandria in Egypt, were covered after firing by a thick lime wash on which the paint was applied. Most of the types and motifs conform to general Hellenistic taste

44 (*Left*) Two terracotta figurines of the 'Tanagra' class, a man and a woman tightly draped with small heads and lean bodies. Both from Amathus and probably made in Cyprus in the 3rd century BC. Ht (of woman) 21 cm.

inspired by mainland Greece, with the eastern influence mainly forgotten. Loose inexpressive forms are concealed by over-elaborate drapery. a *chiton* and *himation* for the women, a large cloak for the men. The finest examples belong to the 'Tanagra' group, which takes its name from the site in Boeotia in northern Greece where such pieces were first found, although it is now clear that the style developed in Athens, whence it spread to all corners of the Hellenistic world. Both men and women have small heads and lean bodies and are tightly draped. The women typically have their hair arranged in the 'melon coiffure', divided on the crown into segments and combed into a bun at the back.

The sculpture of Roman Cyprus comprises a typical mixture of large draped statues, portraits of the different emperors and copies of Greek originals. Statues of rulers and gods were now erected everywhere and adorned public buildings. The tradition of working in 'limestone' continued, and in this medium were the draped statues in the traditional *chiton*, with the *himation* now forming a roll around the waist and falling almost vertically down from the shoulder. The later examples (*c.* AD 130–150) show much use of the drill and a polishing of smooth surfaces in imitation of marble statues. Marble had indeed become much more common. The material must have been imported, but it remains uncertain whether the finished products were carved locally by skilled Cypriots or itinerant sculptors, or else arrived ready-made from the major sculpture workshops in Asia Minor or Greece. A woman's head from Salamis of the second century AD has the heavy facial proportions typical of that era. After AD 250 the Hellenistic realistic tradition broke down, and this resulted in less rational representations of the anatomy and sometimes more expressive gestures. Very little sculpture dating from this time has been found in Cyprus.

6 Jewellery

47 (*Far right, top*) Two gold dress-pins with ornamental heads. The upper part of the shank of the right-hand example, topped by a faience bead, is formed from a double loop-in-loop chain: a western Asiatic type modified by Cypriot jewellers. From Enkomi, *c*.14th century BC. L (of longest) 13.2 cm.

48 (*Far right, bottom*) Gold finger-ring with cloisonné enamel decoration surrounded by two rows of granulation on the bezel. From Old Paphos, 1200–1150 BC. D 2.2 cm.

The ancient Cypriots delighted in sumptuous jewellery. In the fourth century BC their kings gained a reputation for soft living and ostentatious displays of wealth, including the use of purple fabrics: flax was an important crop. This finds echoes in the remains of cloth with purple and gold thread found in a Hellenistic tomb in a necropolis of Salamis near Enkomi. Salamis was the home of Akesas and his son Helikon, who at that time were considered the foremost weavers of their day. A certain Hebdomaios describes himself as a fisher of murex shellfish (which would have provided the purple dye) on a monument set up to his mother at Marion around 300 BC. Jewellery was worn by the first inhabitants on the island, and from early times representations of human figures were adorned with elaborate ornaments.

Most of the raw materials for jewellery came from the east. Gold became plentiful in the Late Bronze Age, when Egypt and Syria were the principal sources. Following Alexander's conquest of the Persian Empire in the fourth century BC, gold again became widely available in the eastern Mediterranean. Asia Minor was a major supplier of silver to the ancient world. Cyprus may also have obtained some from mainland Greek mines, particularly in the fifth century BC when the exceptionally rich vein at Laurion in Attica was discovered and intensively worked.

Precious raw materials reached the craftsmen as 'dumps' (blocks). Most of these dumps were fashioned either into sheet metal by hammering over an anvil or into wire, normally by hammering out, or occasionally by twisting a strip cut from the block and rolling

46 (*Right*) Jewellery of the Late Bronze Age from Cyprus: **a**) a pair of gold earrings, the wire hoops threaded with bulls' heads; **b**) a pair of gold earrings in the form of tapered hoops; **c**) a pair of gold earrings with clusters of beads (the 'mulberry' type); **d**) a gold pendant in the form of a pomegranate; **e**) a necklace of beads of cornelian and gold, including sixteen in the form of double shields. L (of necklace) 35 cm.

it between plates until it reached the required thickness. Charcoal fires provided the heat needed for processes like soldering (joining pieces together by melting) annealing (strengthening by exposure to heat) and casting in moulds. Sheet metal was often embossed: either in the repoussé technique when patterns were formed freehand by hammering from the back; or by stamping, a technique that enabled a pattern to be repeated with the aid of specially made punches applied to the front or the back. Forms were reproduced by working sheet metal into moulds of bronze, terracotta or wood, or by hammering it over a removable core. Wire might be made into finger-rings, hair-rings, earrings, bracelets, pins or *fibulae* (brooches). Wire also formed straps and chains, which played a vital role in jewellery-making. Granulation (attaching grains of precious metals to the surface) and filigree (applying wire) were among the principal decorative processes. Patterns on items of both sheet metal and wire could be incised, traced (a process by which metal was displaced) or engraved (when metal was actually removed). Gold or silver plating was achieved by pressing foil over a core of some other material. In gilding, gold leaf was normally attached by adhesive. The addition of enamel (coloured glass fused to a metallic base) and the inlay of coloured stones and glass gave a polychrome effect.

The early communities wore necklaces of locally available dentalium shells and beads of cornelian that came from the east (p.23). In the Chalcolithic period picrolite (a soft soap-like stone) was used to make pendants. These were often in the form of human figures shaped like a cross similar to many of the larger figurines in the same material (p.34). Groups of dentalium shells were still used for necklaces. An important innovation around 2500 BC was the use of seals of stone apparently to stamp pottery or personal items. This was a short-lived practice not revived until about a thousand years later.

Metal was very occasionally used for jewellery from shortly before 2000 BC. A century later faience (glazed powdered quartz) was imported from Egypt to make beads. As we have already seen (p.18), metal dress-pins now became quite widely used.

It was in the Late Bronze Age that gold became common, imported from the east along with most other raw materials. The east, Egypt and Mycenaean Greece provided some finished products but more often introduced techniques, types and decorative motifs, which were adopted and adapted by Cypriot craftsmen. Granulation was learnt from Mycenaean Greece, but Cypriot innovations probably included the loop-in-loop chain and the use of gold wire, either as applied decoration or to form beads and rings. In form the dress-pins and funerary diadems and mouth-pieces are eastern, but the stamped decoration on the funerary pieces is often of Mycenaean Greek inspiration, while several of the pins incorporate the Cypriot loop-in-loop chain. The finger-rings with decorated bezels have the bezel in line with the hoop in Egyptian fashion (in Mycenaean Greece and Minoan Crete the bezel was set at right angles to the hoop), but the decorative motifs are Mycenaean or peculiarly Cypriot. The swivel finger-ring was another Egyptian invention, although it probably reached Cyprus by way of Syria and Palestine. The finger-rings with circular bezels filled with coloured glass are a Mycenaean Greek type. Particularly popular in Cyprus and probably a local invention were earrings with pendants in the form of bulls' heads. Other styles of earrings such as the tapered hoop and 'mulberry' (decorated with a cluster of beads) were of eastern origin. First made in Cyprus about 1400 BC, they remained popular right until the Archaic period. Necklaces made up of beads of mixed foreign and

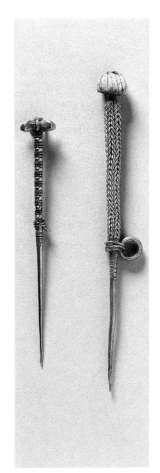

local origin illustrate the amalgam of influences in Late Bronze Age Cyprus.

A long version of the tapered hoop, which was more or less leech-shaped and adapted from a Syrian design, was worn in the twelfth century. Also new at this time, and indeed unknown before in the Bronze Age Greek world, was true cloisonné enamelling. This process involved forming cloisons (cells) by soldering thin strips of metal to the background and filling them with enamel. This technique is used for the decoration of the bezels of gold rings, which in other respects are similar to those with circular bezels inlaid simply with coloured glass. Since, therefore, the technique is new but the form is not, it seems likely that they were made either by an immigrant craftsman or a Cypriot who had learnt this skill abroad, perhaps in Egypt. To the eleventh century BC belong gold versions of the D-shaped *fibula*, originally introduced from the Bronze Age Greek world. Another innovation is the manufacture of gold plaques of eastern design, which would have formed tiara-like headdresses (*poloi*). Other plaques are simply decorated with rosettes. These jewellery designs continued throughout the next three centuries.

In the Archaic period (750–475 BC) the jewellery for the most part continued the types that were now well established in the Cypriot repertoire, although techniques improved and the decoration was more elaborate, often enriched with fine granulation. Connections were established with craftsmen in the Greek east: in the seventh century BC Cyprus introduced the gold embossed plaques to Rhodes and common both in Cyprus and at Ephesus were earrings with 'boat-shaped' hollow hoops to which the pins were attached. These earrings were of Syrian origin but it is not clear whether the Cypriot examples were made locally or imported from East Greece. Also in the seventh century BC other types of earrings,

the tapered hoop and the 'mulberry' which had survived in Cyprus through the 'Dark Age', were re-introduced to the Greek world.

A new series of gems, which were often set in rings and used like sealstones to impress the owner's mark on documents and possessions, began in the Greek world around 580 BC. These were made of hardstones in the form of an Egyptian scarab beetle, and the decoration was engraved with a drill and a wheel. This art was learnt by the Greeks from the Phoenicians, probably in Cyprus, where the two communities lived side by side. The many gems of the later sixth and earlier fifth centuries found in Cyprus, several of which bear Cypriot inscriptions, suggest that the Greek Cypriot workshops continued in existence, although their products in both their subject matter and style are similar to those from Greek island and Ionian workshops. The Semon Master, who was active between about 500 and 480 BC and was one of the two major artists of the late Archaic period, may have worked in Cyprus.

Filigree became more popular than granulation in the Classical period, and enamel, sometimes bordered by filigree, was used for inlay. Silver became common (perhaps now obtained from Greece) and gold-plated bronze was the medium favoured by Cypriot jewellers. Popular in Cyprus and probably made

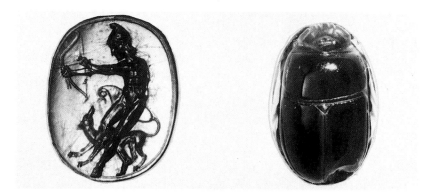

49 Two gems from Cyprus: (*left*) a plasma scaraboid by the Semon Master showing a youth drawing his bow accompanied by his dog, 500–480 BC; (*right*) the back of a cornelian gem, in the form of a scarab beetle, from Amathus, 550–500 BC.

50 Gold jewellery of the Hellenistic period from Cyprus dating from the late 4th and 3rd centuries BC: **a**) a pendant from a necklace with two figures of Eros perching on a rosette; **b**) a pair of earrings of twisted wire terminating in lions' heads; **c**) a chain necklace with a lion's head at each end; one of the lions holds a 'Herakles' (reef) knot in its mouth L (of necklace) 31.3 cm.

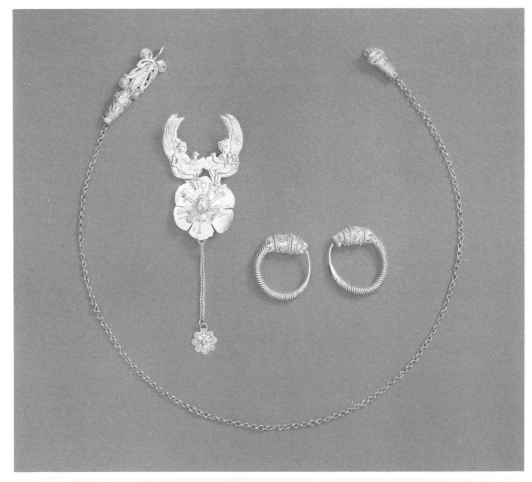

51 Hellenistic and Roman finger-rings from Cyprus: **a**) (*top right*) a gold ring-setting with sunken relief decoration showing the sanctuary of Aphrodite at Old Paphos, 2nd to 3rd century AD; **b**) (*top left*) the same scene and a goddess (Isis) engraved on a gold ring with a double bezel, 2nd to 3rd century AD; **c**) (*bottom left*) a gilded bronze ring with a glass setting, late 4th century BC; **d**) (*bottom right*) a gold ring with two sapphire settings, 3rd to 4th century AD. D (of **d**) 2.3 cm.

locally were bracelets with open ends terminating in animal heads, and others in the form of snakes. Both of these varieties were known earlier in the Greek world. Other favourite types probably made locally included spiral rings; more suitable for the hair than the ears, they terminate in female or animal heads. The heads are worked in repoussé and attached to the spiral by collars with filigree ornament that sometimes outline enamel inlays. Gold pendants were often in the form of vases or acorns, the latter sometimes made of cornelian with a gold cap. Intricate pieces of pure gold, such as earrings with fine filigree decoration, were probably imported from Greece.

Personal jewellery was plentiful in Hellenistic and Roman Cyprus, although since Cypriot craftsmen followed cosmopolitan fashions it is often unclear whether individual items were made locally or imported. Techniques were generally unelaborate, and both filigree and granulation became rare. A new polychrome style was achieved by the addition of coloured stones and glass.

In the Hellenistic period (325–30 BC) some finger-rings became mounts for engraved or precious stones or glass set in large bezels. They indicated the official status of the owner. Snake finger-rings were common throughout the eastern Mediterranean but Cyprus imported her glass finger-rings from Syrian workshops. Earrings of twisted wire, sometimes threaded with coloured beads and with elaborate terminals, were perhaps a Cypriot creation. A new motif, the 'Herakles knot', was adopted throughout the Hellenistic world from Egypt. Eros was a favourite motif on the island. Jewellery found in Cyprus at this time, like chain necklaces terminating in a Herakles knot or animal heads and earrings with pendants, are also common elsewhere.

Hellenistic traditions continued into the early Roman period. The ostentatious finger-rings now signified the military status of the wearer. A change came about after the second century AD with the introduction of the piercing of gold in a kind of network technique and the more abundant use of coloured stones. Many rather plain types of earrings were produced. Necklaces of chains or straps now often incorporated the popular wheel motif, but others were more simply composed of gold links with semi-precious stones or glass beads. Of local manufacture were the finger-rings with engraved and sunken relief decoration on the bezels sold as souvenirs to pilgrims visiting the sanctuary of Aphrodite at Old Paphos. It is clear, therefore, that Cypriot jewellers remained active even into late antiquity and continued to manufacture at least some truly 'Cypriot' items.

52 (*Left*) Jewellery of the Roman period from Cyprus dating to the 2nd or 3rd centuries AD: **a**) a pair of gold earrings with glass settings; **b**) two gold earrings (not a pair) with pendants; **c**) a gold necklace with garnet beads and a wheel motif with garnet settings in the centre. L (of necklace) 33 cm.

53 (*Right*) Red Polished plank-shaped figurine cradling a child; a fertility charm. 19th–18th century BC. Ht 26 cm.

7 Religion and burial customs

To recreate the religious beliefs and practices of a past civilisation is notoriously difficult. The lack of documentary evidence in the form of inscribed representations naming the deity or descriptive texts makes the task even harder. Burial customs are easier to unravel. Tombstones and sarcophagi (coffins) and, more importantly, many of the actual graves survive, still containing the goods given to the dead to accompany them to the next world. These grave gifts are sometimes the principal evidence for the material culture of a particular period.

Religious beliefs and practices

37

The beliefs of prehistoric Cyprus remain obscure, but the concept of fertility was evidently paramount. Whether the early human figurines of the stump and cruciform varieties (p. 34) are to be identified as fertility charms or fertility goddesses, in practical terms their function would have been the same. These religious beliefs continued even though in the Late Bronze Age (1650–1050 BC), greater foreign influence is apparent in both representations and practice. The new Syrian type of female figurine is often described as the 'Astarte' type, taking the name of the eastern mother goddess. However, as this identification of such figurines found in their homeland is far from certain, doubt must also remain over the assumption that the Cypriot examples are goddesses.

The earliest sanctuary remains are of this period. The first were built in the later fifteenth century BC. The major period of construction was around 1200 BC, while worship continued in some of the earlier foundations into the twelfth century. Most were close to settlements, and some to copper workshops. Several represent a Near Eastern type of court sanctuary consisting of a walled *temenos* (open

court), with a small covered 'holy of holies' or other cult buildings. The altar, often crowned by handmade bulls' horns, known as 'horns of consecration', usually stood in the open air. Worship occasionally took place in rooms within larger structures.

Some idea of the religious customs can be learnt from the objects discovered in these sanctuaries. Practices like the wearing of anthropomorphic masks and the offering of models of kidneys apparently used in divination mirror customs known earlier in Syria and Palestine. Among the dedications were small copper ingots and remarkable bronze statuettes. The last included a horned male figure and a female 'Astarte', with her hands held at her breasts, both standing on ingots. They must represent protectors, perhaps divine, of the copper industry. In the sanctuaries of these 'horned gods' quantities of horned animals were sacrificed and animal masks were apparently worn. Both here and elsewhere libations were offered.

back cover

The typical sanctuary of the earlier Iron Age combined a walled *temenos* with small cult buildings and altars. The larger cities had several shrines, nearly all situated away from the settlements to which they belonged, although the sacred precincts of the Phoenician Astarte at Kition-Kathari and of Aphrodite-Astarte and Cybele at Tamassos were close to copper workshops. Soloi and the neighbouring town of Paradisotissa had small temples on the Greek plan with *pronaos* and *cella*, but these were very rare in Cyprus until a much later date.

Although there is some documentary evidence for the gods worshipped in Archaic and Classical Cyprus (750–325 BC), very few of the surviving representations are actually named, so the identification of individual statues of gods and goddesses remains problematical.

The principal deity was the Great Mother Goddess. She was identified above all with

Aphrodite, the Cypriot goddess *par excellence*, who was already described as 'the Cyprian' in the eighth-century BC poems of Homer and the slightly later works of Hesiod. Her sanctuary at Old Paphos was the chief religious centre of the island and famous throughout the ancient Mediterranean world. The early Greek writers call her Aphrodite, while dedications in other sanctuaries in Cyprus in the sixth century BC name her simply 'the Paphian'. At Old Paphos itself the first dedicatory inscriptions are of the fourth century BC. In these she is simply called 'Wanassa', the 'lady'. This is a very old title, perhaps known already in Linear B texts from Mycenaean Greece. It apparently signifies the great antiquity of the cult. At Old Paphos too she was represented by a conical stone, obviously a symbol of fertility as in many other oriental and Mediterranean cults. This aniconic worship of Aphrodite was, however, peculiar to Paphos. Among the offerings made in the sanctuary in the Archaic period are many terracotta figurines of women wearing tall hats and with their arms upraised. These may represent either the goddess herself or her worshippers. If they are indeed representations of the goddess offered by worshippers, there would be reason to identify all the Cypriot representations of women in tall hats or crowns as Aphrodite. Raising the arms is a well-known gesture of worship, but some scholars argue for the introduction of a cult of a 'goddess with uplifted arms' from Crete in the eleventh century BC. The true answer to these questions may never be known. However, whatever interpretation is given to the many female figures from sanctuaries, it is clear that the worship of a fertility goddess remained supreme in Cyprus.

Cypriot gods included a principal male deity and various local gods, including one of the woodland (Hylates) and another of music, perhaps the deified Kinyras, the legendary founder and first king of Paphos.

54 (*Left*) Painted terracotta figurine of a woman with her arms upraised, bedecked with jewellery and wearing a *polos* (tall hat); a worshipper or a fertility goddess, perhaps Aphrodite herself. From the sanctuary of Aphrodite at Old Paphos, 7th century BC. Ht 36 cm.

55 (*Right*) Terracotta figurines of the Egyptian dwarf gods 'Bes', bearded and with leonine features, and Ptah. Their cults were introduced to Cyprus by the Phoenicians. Both were made in the 6th century BC and were found at Amathus. Ht (of 'Bes') 17 cm.

The Phoenicians introduced their own deities. Of their pantheon, there is documentary evidence in Cyprus for the worship of the goddesses Astarte and Anat, and the gods Baal, Eshmoun, Reshef, Mikal, Melqart and Shed. Egyptian cults of 'Bes', Ptah, Hathor and Thoeris were introduced by the Phoenicians early in the Archaic period, before the time of Egyptian rule. Small representations of these particular deities were often made into charms to ward off evil. From about 500 BC Hathor may have been identified with Aphrodite. A single dedication to Isis on a bronze jug offered 'to the god' at Kourion is evidence for direct Egyptian influence during the years of Egyptian domination.

There is difficulty again in naming anonymous representations of some of these deities. Figures of a horned 'god' with a human or ram's head, seated on a throne supported by rams, have been identified as Baal-Hamman

56 Limestone statuette wearing a lionskin and holding a lion in his left hand. His right arm was originally upraised and held a club at his forehead. Reminiscent of both the Phoencian god Melqart and the Greek hero Herakles, he may have been known in Cyprus by the name of another Phoenician deity, Reshef-Mikal. From the sanctuary of Apollo at Idalion, 5th century BC. Ht 60 cm.

('god of the perfume altar'), whose worship is also attested in Phoenician colonies in the western Mediterranean. Ram cults were quite common in Cypriot rustic shrines and must have been influenced, too, by the Libyan ram god, Ammon. Popular dedications in sanctuaries of Astarte in both Phoenicia and Cyprus were terracotta figurines of pregnant women, which at least confirm her role as a fertility goddess. It is uncertain by what name the Cypriots knew statues of a male figure dressed in a tunic covered by a lionskin, brandishing a club in one hand and holding a lion in the other. The representations, most of which are of the fifth and fourth centuries BC, are reminiscent of both the Phoenician Melqart and the Greek Herakles, but in Cyprus he may have been called Reshef (or Reshef-Mikal) or Apollo.

There is no firm evidence that the worship of Greek deities was established in Cyprus before the fourth century BC, with the exception of fifth-century cults of Athena at Idalion and Vouni. The cult of Zeus at Salamis had the reputation for great antiquity. Literary texts of the Roman period claim that it dates from the foundation of the city in the eleventh century BC. In this they echo a comment by an Athenian orator writing around 374–365 BC, which confirms its existence in the fourth century but not necessarily earlier. A 'great god' was certainly worshipped at Salamis from an early date, but whether he was known as Zeus equally early remains uncertain.

It was in the fourth century BC that Greek cults became widespread in the island. At this time too Cypriot and Phoenician gods and goddesses started to become identified with Greek deities. The principal god may henceforth have been known as Zeus, at least at Salamis. The Cypriot Hylates and the Phoenician Reshef both became identified with the Greek Apollo. There were many local cults of Apollo in Cyprus. At Tamassos there is mention in an inscription of the fourth century BC

of Apollo Alasiotas, Apollo of Alasia. While tempting to see this as evidence of an ancient cult of a 'god of Alasia', which would help to confirm the identification of Cyprus with Alasia, the *Alashiya* or *Asy* of the Near Eastern texts (p.19), it is possible that the epithet 'of Alasia' refers to a foreign deity, although no dedications to him have yet been recorded outside the island. At Pyla there was an Apollo Keraeatas, Apollo of the horns, but it is difficult to see in this a reflection of a Late Bronze Age cult of horned gods, which itself is not assured. At this time too the Cypriot Aphrodite became identified with the Phoenician Astarte (although at Old Paphos this did not happen until the third century BC) and Anat. Anat was also identified with the Greek Athena, while at Kition the cult of the Phoenician Eshmoun became the cult of the Greek Asklepios. The Greek huntress goddess, Artemis, was also worshipped and the Kitians established a cult of their own, Artemis Paralia (Artemis of the sea-coast). In their final years in the late fourth century BC some of the kings of the cities made strenuous efforts to Hellenise their kingdoms, and in so doing propagated Greek cults. Dedications were now made for the first time to Hera and also to Demeter and Kore.

In the Archaic and Classical periods the sanctuaries were hives of activity. Here the gods were believed to reside and even participate in the sacred banquets accompanied by ritual dancing celebrated in their honour. The priests wore animal and anthropomorphic masks, animals (and occasionally humans) were sacrificed, libations were offered and incense burnt. The offerings included many statues and statuettes of limestone and terracotta (and occasionally of bronze) which the devotees believed acted as substitutes for themselves as continuous worshippers. Some idea of the identity of the deity may be gained from the dedications; in the sanctuaries of gods statuettes of horsemen and chariots are com-

57 Terracotta group of figurines of worshippers or priests putting on bulls' masks in preparation for a religious ceremony. There were originally five figures in the group, but only two are preserved. From the sanctuary of Apollo at Kourion, 650–600 BC. Ht 9.7 cm.

58 Group of musicians representing participants in a religious ceremony accompanying sacred dances; **a**) a terracotta female lyre-player bedecked with jewellery and wearing a tunic with a sash, from Achna; **b**) a limestone figure playing pipes, from Tamassos; **c**) a limestone female tambourine-player wearing a long tunic decorated with red painted stripes, from Amathus. 6th century BC. Ht (of lyre-player) 39 cm.

mon while in those of the fertility goddess bearers of offerings, mostly women, worshippers (or the goddess herself) with upraised arms and musicians predominate. Locks of hair were offered to the Phoenician goddess Astarte. Sacred prostitution in the cults of Aphrodite at Old Paphos and of Astarte at Kition is recorded in certain texts. At Kition it is said to have involved women and young boys. This may provide an explanation for the dedication of statues of small boys ('temple boys') which continued into the Hellenistic period. A pair of terracotta statuettes of boys completely naked were dedicated to Eshmoun in his sanctuary near Sidon (Phoenicia) around 330 BC. This suggests that sacred prostitution was another Phoenician or oriental trait in Cypriot religion. A 'master of the water' is described as presiding over the dispensing of libations at Kition.

Cyprus' religious institutions were naturally affected by Ptolemaic rule. From the early second century BC the *strategos* received the title of High Priest, which enabled him to collect the revenues from all the sanctuaries and so enrich the royal coffers. The worship of the ruling Ptolemy, the Dynastic cult, became of prime importance. A special organisation known as the '*Koinon* (confederation) of Cypriots' was set up to promote it. However, existing religious practices were scarcely interfered with and worship continued at many of the traditional open sanctuaries and rustic shrines. In the third century BC many dedications were made to a nymph in a remote hilltop shrine at Kaphizin (near Nicosia), where she may already have been worshipped for many centuries. Being Greeks themselves, the Ptolemies promoted Greek cults. Greek deities worshipped included Zeus, Apollo, Dionysos, Pan or Melanthios, Poseidon, Asklepios (and Hygeia), Athena, Hera and Artemis. Aphrodite remained the supreme goddess, now more often identified with Astarte,

59 Limestone statue of a crouching child wearing rich jewellery and holding a rabbit beside him in his left hand. Commonly known as 'temple boys', these statues were often dedicated in sanctuaries in Cyprus. They may represent temple servants or prostitutes, or simply commemorate the occasion when the boy made his first offering in the sanctuary. From the sanctuary of Apollo at Idalion, *c.* 300 BC. Ht 41 cm.

60 Part of the sanctuary of Aphrodite at Old Paphos on a bronze coin of Cyprus issued under the Roman emperor Caracalla (AD 198–217). Her dove feeds in the courtyard in front of the building, and there are more doves on the roof. The cult image, in the central tower, is a conical stone.

whose cult survived. Frequently identified with Aphrodite was Arsinoe, the wife of Ptolemy II Philadelphus (285–245 BC), deified on her death in 270 BC. Her cult enjoyed particular popularity in Cyprus and may well have started during her lifetime. Cities were founded in her name, including one on the former site of Marion, which had been destroyed in 312 BC. The Ptolemies also introduced cults of Egyptian deities, including Serapis and Isis. Some Egyptian gods were equated with Greek deities, as Zeus was with the Libyan Ammon.

Dedications continued in many of the open sanctuaries. Some were constructed like those to Aphrodite and Serapis and Isis near Soloi and others were rebuilt, as was the sanctuary of Astarte–Aphrodite and Cybele at Tamassos. Inscriptions record the construction of temples in the cities, but their remains seldom survive. An exception is the temple of Zeus at Salamis. An example of the Greco-Roman type, it was built on a podium in the second century BC.

Having worshipped their Ptolemaic rulers, the Cypriots found no difficulty in transferring their loyalty to the Roman emperors. The Imperial cult was as important as the Dynastic cult had been. The *Koinon* became an officially recognised central organisation. Its headquarters were at the sanctuary of Aphrodite at Old Paphos which was now joined by a sacred way to the new city. One of its principal functions was to promote the worship of the Roman emperors. Some of the traditional rites survived, as did the worship of Greek deities. The cult of the Paphian Aphrodite remained 60 pre-eminent. Musical and literary contests were among the popular ceremonies at her annual feast. As in the Hellenistic period there are many more temples recorded in inscriptions than actually survive. The temple of Zeus at Salamis was rebuilt. Traditional sanctuaries were remodelled and enlarged but the earlier cult place was always included in the new design. At Curium (Kourion) and Amathus a classic Greco-Roman temple became the focal point of the redesigned sanctuary, but at Old Paphos the basic Near Eastern plan remained.

Her geographical position and the presence of a strong Jewish community meant that Cyprus was one of the first areas of Christian mission. Paul and Barnabas (a native of Salamis) visited the island in AD 45. The island did not, however, fully embrace Christianity until it became the official religion of the Roman Empire in the late fourth century AD.

Burial customs

Inhumation was the normal funerary rite in ancient Cyprus. Cremation occurred only rarely, as a result of foreign contact. The first settlers buried their dead under the floors of their houses or in pits outside. Pit graves continued to be the usual type of tomb in the Chalcolithic period (4000/3900–2500 BC), although there was now more variety, including the appearance of a new bottle-shaped type of deep pit in western Cyprus. Towards the end of the period the same region provides evidence of practices foreshadowing Bronze Age customs: the pit graves were now occasionally set apart from settlements in cemeteries and, even more rarely, the dead were accompanied by gifts. A few rock-cut chamber tombs are also known, but these have hitherto only been found under houses inside a settlement.

The real changes in practice occurred soon after 2500 BC. Tombs were now normally cut in the rock; the dead were buried in irregularly shaped chambers approached by short pit-like entrance passages (*dromoi*). The graves were regularly in cemeteries, away from the settlements, and the dead were accompanied by gifts. The same tomb might be used on more than one occasion. With some variations, this type of tomb and these customs were the most common throughout the Bronze Age.

Variations from the norm included the reappearance of bottle-shaped pits with no entrance passages in a cemetery in the southwest in the later third millennium. In some cemeteries of the seventeenth century BC a rather different type of tomb occurs, with a kidney-shaped chamber approached by stairs in a long, wedge-shaped passage.

At Enkomi and also at Old Paphos in the Late Bronze Age the dead were again buried under the houses. Most common are the normal rock-cut chamber tombs, but at Enkomi there are some tombs of a different construction. These must have been for the wealthy or ruling class. It may be significant that the earliest (of the sixteenth century BC) has a conical roof, like an old-fashioned beehive, built of stone blocks, similar to the 'tholos' tombs of Mycenaean Greece, but the others have no close parallels in the Bronze Age Greek world.

In cemeteries of the eleventh century BC rock-cut tombs of the Mycenaean Greek type,

61 A typical rock-cut chamber tomb approached by a *dromos* (entrance passage) of the early Archaic period; in the Xylinos cemetery at Old Paphos.

with long narrow *dromoi* and rectangular chambers, occur alongside the traditional Cypriot variety. Cremation, as in the Greek world, was practised, as well as the more usual inhumation. Together, the new type of tomb and the cremation of some of the dead confirm the arrival of Greek colonists in Cyprus by this time.

Rock-cut chamber tombs, with wider 61 *dromoi* and many minor variations in overall plan, remained the normal grave for the ordinary people until the end of the Roman era. But for the aristocracy of the city–kingdoms tombs were being constructed on a larger scale. At Salamis monumental tombs, their façades crowned by Egyptian cavetto cornices, were built in the late eighth and seventh centuries BC. They had extremely wide entrance passages to accommodate the wheeled vehicles which transported the dead to burial. The vehicles were drawn by horses or donkeys, which were then sacrificed to accompany the dead to the other world. In the richest of the tombs ten vehicles were discovered; the draught animals had bronze harnesses and trappings. The grave goods were exceptionally rich, including bronze vessels and furniture with ivory fittings. All these items were imported from different parts of the Near East or, if made locally, show strong eastern influence. They constitute an appropriate display of finery for a despot living on the western fringe of the Assyrian Empire. A set of thirty-three Greek vases in another tomb may be evidence for an exchange of gifts between Greek and Cypriot noble families. In other tombs cattle and, perhaps, a slave or prisoner were sacrificed and amphorae containing olive oil were offered. Iron spits have also been found, associated with fire-dogs, recalling the kitchen gear of heroes in the epic poems of Homer. One tomb was finally covered by a huge mound, and there are a few cases of cremation. Some scholars have seen these tombs and their customs as mirroring the burial practices described in Homer's poems. If so, they may have been inspired by the epic poetry which was circulating in the eighth century BC. Otherwise, they may simply represent a continuation of Mycenaean Greek practices, albeit after a considerable time-gap. This gap has been partly filled by the recent discovery of a heroic burial of the mid-tenth century BC at Lefkandi in Euboea.

Fine stone-built tombs of the seventh and sixth centuries BC have been discovered at the sites of other city–kingdoms, including Tamassos, Idalion, Kition, Amathus and Soloi. A few occur elsewhere, as at Patriki and Trachonas. The finest are those at Tamassos, whose architecture in stone imitates wooden construction. Certain details are of Phoenician origin. The *dromos* of a simple rock-cut chamber tomb in the same cemetery contained the remains of horses that had been sacrificed, their bronze trappings and a bronze helmet recalling the practices at Salamis.

For the cult of the dead evidence comes from another cemetery at Salamis, which was in use from around 700 to 300 BC. Pyres were discovered close by or actually in the *dromoi* of simple rock-cut tombs. In the ashes were a number of offerings, all burnt, including vases evidently smashed after a libation had been offered. A similar custom was practised in Athens, but there the pyres were associated with cremation. In the same cemetery at Salamis children were buried in vessels, either Phoenician jars or amphorae of Cypriot or Greek manufacture. This was a very ancient burial rite, which may have been adopted by the Cypriots from Phoenicia, since only Phoenician jars were used for the burial of children in the town of Salamis between the eleventh and eighth centuries BC.

On the outskirts of another cemetery at Salamis a short rock-cut *dromos* leads to a burial chamber with a vaulted roof and paved floor. The whole of the interior of the chamber carries painted decoration exactly like the inside of an Egyptian sarcophagus. Belonging to the middle years of the sixth century BC, this is evidence of direct influence from Egypt during the period of Egyptian rule.

In the Classical period burial customs changed little, although sarcophagi, known only rarely earlier, became more common. Simple versions, carved from solid blocks or made of slabs fitted together, were used in ordinary graves. More elaborate examples with fine relief decoration were made for aristocrats or 80 kings early in the period, and later marble mummy-shaped coffins were imported from Phoenicia. Phoenicians at Kition made their own mummy-shaped sarcophagi locally. A Cypriot-made example from Amathus shows only the head, and keeps specifically Cypriot 62 features. From this period too graves were more often marked by tombstones or statues.

Ptolemaic and Roman rule had little effect on established practices, except that niches and *loculi* (larger rectangular extensions) were cut into some chamber tombs to enlarge the accommodation for the dead and their gifts. Some of the dead were buried in simple shafts or pits. Rock-cut subterranean tombs in Hellenistic Paphos are versions of those found at Alexandria in Egypt, and must have served the aristocrats or local rulers. Two rock-cut tombs have painted chambers, recalling the sixth-century BC tomb at Salamis. and are another indication of Alexandrian customs. At Amathus gravestones bear painted decoration. These may again reflect Alexandrian influence, although similar gravestones are also found in northern Greece. Tombstones were generally quite common in the Hellenistic and Roman periods, as were sarcophagi.

Under the Romans in south and central Cyprus cylindrical altar-like *cippi* (small pillars) also marked the graves of the ruling and middle classes. These *cippi* had inscriptions on their shafts, which usually read simply: Dear . . ., child of . . ., fare thee well'. The wealthy were still buried in stone-built tombs. Some were newly constructed but others, including certain of the 'Alexandrian' version at New Paphos, were reused. Roman burials were also made in some Hellenistic rock-cut chamber tombs. The use of the same tomb for more than one generation had a long history on the island, and this must be one of the reasons for the overall conservatism of the burial customs of ancient Cyprus.

62 Limestone sarcophagus, a Cypriot version of an originally Phoenician type of mummy-shaped sarcophagus. The box is rounded at the top and is provided with feet in the Cypriot tradition. On the lid is the head of a bearded man, presumably the occupant. From a tomb at Amathus, *c*.450 BC. L 190 cm.

63 View of the courtyard of one of the subterranean 'tombs of the Kings' carved in the rock for the aristocrats or ruling class at New Paphos in the Hellenistic period. They mirror those in cemeteries in the newly founded city of Alexandria in Egypt.

65 (Above) Limestone grave relief showing the deceased (in the centre), probably with his mother and his brother. The men wear *chitons* (tunics) and *himatia* (cloaks), and the woman has a *chiton*, girded below her breasts and partly covered by a cloak. From Tremithusa, near Golgoi, *c.* 1st century AD. Ht 98.5 cm.

64 (*Left*) Limestone *stele* (gravestone) with painted decoration showing a boy holding a pigeon in his outstretched left hand. Similar stelae are known from Alexandria in Egypt and from northern Greece. Found on the surface above a tomb at Amathus, *c.* third century BC. Ht 69 cm.

8 Coinage

Coins were first manufactured in Cyprus in the late sixth century BC, when the island was organised into several city–kingdoms. As the rulers of these kingdoms at this time all owed allegiance and paid tribute to the Great King of Persia. it is not surprising that when each of the city–kingdoms began to issue coinage they adopted the same weight standard. This weight system is known as the 'Persic' because, although it had originated not in Persia but in western Asia Minor, it was taken over by the Persian conquerors of that region and eventually spread to many parts of the Persian Empire. Despite their use of the same weight system, the coins of the Cypriot city–kingdoms in the Persian period (until 330 BC) varied considerably in choice of designs, artistic style and, because of the mixed origins of the island's population, scripts: Cypriot, Phoenician and Greek.

The earliest Cypriot coins were all made of silver. They were produced by hammering an ingot of metal between two dies; the designs engraved into the dies were thus transferred to the coin. This method of minting is known as striking. At first only the lower die was engraved, but soon the upper 'punch' die was also given a recognisable design. The designs were intended to identify the authority behind the issue of coinage by way of an appropriate pictorial design, sometimes supplemented by an inscription, which would usually appear in abbreviated form. The designs are not as intelligible to us as they would have been to the people for whom the coins were originally produced, and some of the earliest issues of Cyprus have not yet been given precise attributions. Many of the designs on early Cypriot coins were copied from coins produced elsewhere in the Greek world. This is one of the indications that at that time there was considerable movement of silver coinage from the Aegean eastwards to the Persian Empire. Indeed, much Greek coinage is found as bullion in hoards of silver in the east, and these hoards, which are mostly from Eygpt and Syria, often contain Cypriot coins.

The main denomination for Cypriot coinage in the Persian period was the double shekel, weighing about 10.8g, but to make coinage more flexible smaller denominations were also produced. By the late fifth century BC a wide range of small-denomination silver coins were in use on the island, all accurately weighed as fractions of the shekel: thirds, sixths, twelfths, twenty-fourths, and even the tiny forty-eighths, weighing little more than a tenth of a gramme. These smaller fractions would have represented the small change of the day, for buying and selling in the market-place. The British Museum collection contains a number of these pieces from a hoard found at Idalion in 1869.

In the fifth or fourth centuries BC mints were operating in virtually all the major cities of the island: coinages have been attributed to Salamis, Paphos, Kition, Idalion, Amathus, Lapithos and Marion. It is in this period, therefore, that the most varied coinage was produced, and the designs are an important source of information for religion, art and political history. Designs were chosen which symbolised the city–kingdoms or their rulers;

66 The head of an eagle and scroll decoration on a silver coin of an uncertain Cypriot city; c.480 BC.

67 Silver staters of the city-kingdoms: **a**) the ram with disc and crescent on a coin of Salamis (*c*.480 BC) are symbols of the worship of Aphrodite; **b**) a coin of Paphos, with a bull, winged disc and circular symbol of fertility, *c*.430 BC; **c**) a coin of Kition showing Herakles-Melqart with a club and bow, *c*.479–449 BC.

then, once established, the same themes tended to remain on the coinage so that it would be recognised: the ram and *ankh* sign (the Egyptian symbol of life) at Salamis, the bull at Paphos, the sphinx and lotus flower at Idalion, and Herakles-Melqart at Kition, the chief Phoenician city. The island's ethnic and cultural mixture is well illustrated. Coin designs are mostly in the Greek tradition, accompanied usually by Cypriot lettering at Salamis, Paphos, Idalion, Amathus and Marion, and by Phoenician lettering at Kition and Lapithos. Sometimes a cultural mixture is strikingly visible. Lapithos has coins with designs featuring Greek subjects executed in typically Greek style, alongside inscriptions in Phoenician lettering. Political upheavals at Salamis are reflected in the issues of coinage which use first Cypriot lettering, then Phoenician, and then Cypriot alongside Greek.

Some interesting developments can be seen against the background of the struggle between Evagoras I, King of Salamis (411–373 BC), and the Persians. Evagoras, a representative of the Greek Teucrid dynasty, actively promoted Greek culture, and his coins have a notably fine artistic 'Greek' style. He also introduced Greek lettering for coin inscriptions and issued the first gold coins to be produced on the island. Later, under another king of Salamis, Evagoras II (361–351 BC), a further innovation took place when Cyprus' first bronze coinage was minted, providing an alternative to the impractical small silver fractions used for the lowest denominations.

When the Persian Empire was conquered by Alexander the Great (336–323 BC) Cyprus

68 (*Left*) Gold fractions of Evagoras I of Salamis (411–373 BC): **a**) the head of Herakles-Melqart; **b**, **c**) the forepart and head of a goat; **d**) the Cypriot sign BA, signifying the royal title of the king.

was first absorbed into Alexander's empire; then, after Alexander's death, the island was fought over in the wars between his successors – Ptolemy, and Antigonus the One-Eyed, with his son Demetrius the Besieger. One of the most interesting coinages of this period was issued by Demetrius after his victory over Ptolemy in a sea battle off Salamis in 306 BC. The coins, some of which were minted at Salamis, depict Victory blowing a trumpet on the prow of a galley. Eventually, though, Ptolemy prevailed and Cyprus became a long-term possession of the Ptolemaic kings of Egypt.

The character of Cyprus' coinage was completely transformed by these dramatic historical developments. With the effective disappearance of the city–kingdoms the individuality seen in the earlier coinage issues was lost. From the time of Alexander the cities of Cyprus which still produced coins became merely branch mints issuing coins for local circulation as part of a monetary system controlled from outside. The city's identity was often reduced to a mere symbol or initial, subsidiary to the major coin type. Worth mentioning is a series of silver tetradrachms issued with the usual designs and in the name of Alexander the Great by Nikokles, the last

king of Paphos in the 320s, on which the name of the local king is inscribed, secretively, in minute letters among the hairs of the lion scalp worn by Herakles.

Under the Ptolemies only four cities are identified as mints: Kition, Paphos, Salamis and Amathus. They produced issues in silver and occasionally also gold, which are virtually identical to the Egyptian series. They are distinguishable only by initials included within the design to identify the minting cities. These issues, which were mostly struck in the second century BC, can be dated precisely because the year of the reign is also included in the design, in Greek numerals prefixed by the letter L, a convention derived from Ptolemaic Egypt. Cyprus also produced issues of bronze coinage under the Ptolemies, though these cannot be attributed to individual mints. Some coins depicted the Cypriot goddess Aphrodite, others have designs simply copying the Ptolemaic bronze coins of Egypt.

Cyprus was ruled by the Ptolemies until 58 BC, when it became a Roman province, though for a brief period during Rome's civil wars the island was restored to the Ptolemies (47–30 BC). The coinage issued by Cleopatra VII in Cyprus at this time includes an interesting bronze coin depicting Cleopatra with her child,

69 The victory of Demetrius the Besieger off Salamis in 306 BC inspired the design of this silver tetradrachm. On the obverse Victory blows her trumpet on the prow of the war-galley; on the reverse Poseidon hurls his trident.

70 (*Left*) Cleopatra and her baby Caesarion, son of Julius Caesar, on a Cypriot bronze coin (44–30 BC). The Ptolemies of Egypt regularly struck coins for use within the island.

71 (*Left*) The cult figure of Zeus of Salamis on a Cypriot bronze coin of the emperor Vespasian (AD 69–79): the reverse of 13. He is shown with his eagle, and is pouring a libation.

the son of Julius Caesar. After the Battle of Actium and Cleopatra's death in 30 BC the island reverted to Rome.

The first coinage produced in Cyprus under Roman rule dates from the reign of Augustus (31 BC–AD 14). Until after Claudius' reign (AD 41–54) only bronze coins were minted on the island, and indeed this was usual for most eastern provinces of the Empire: production of silver coinage was confined to a few major centres, while numerous cities produced bronze 'Greek imperials'. Like most provincial coinages, the issues of Cyprus always portrayed a head of the emperor, or other member of the imperial family, on at least one side of the coin. The earliest Cypriot issues of the Roman period have inscriptions in Latin, but from the time of Claudius Greek was invariably used, as with most 'Greek imperial' coins.

Some of the early issues of the Roman province were signed by the governor; others have no inscriptions that clearly link them with Cyprus, but they can be identified as Cypriot either because of their reverse designs, depicting the sanctuary of Aphrodite at Old Paphos or the cult figure of Zeus of Salamis, or on the evidence of finds from the island. Under Claudius the first issues signed by the provincial council (Koinon) appear. Paphos, which was now the principal city in Cyprus, was the seat of the Koinon and it is presumed that most of the Koinon issues would have been minted there.

In the reign of Vespasian (AD 69–79) Cyprus was provided with a brief issue of silver coinage, together with related bronze coins, dated by the emperor's regnal years to the period 76–9. The bronze coinage was signed by the Koinon of Cyprus, but the silver was not, implying perhaps that it was issued directly by the Roman government, though the designs on the reverses refer again to the island's principal cults: Paphian Aphrodite and Zeus of Salamis. The bronze coins of Vespasian and his

sons from AD 76 to 79, and also those issued in the name of the Koinon under Trajan (AD 98–117), have a style, fabric and metal which suggest they may have been minted at Rome, rather than in Cyprus. They contrast greatly with the earlier bronze coins which have a clearly local, not Roman, style.

Occasional issues only were produced after the reign of Trajan, and these were probably confined to bronze coins. An issue depicting Antoninus Pius (AD 138–161) and Marcus Aurelius Caesar has been attributed to Cyprus because most of the surviving examples have been found on the island. Further issues were produced under Septimius Severus (AD 193–211) and his family; these are now again signed by the Koinon. The last Cypriot coinage of the Roman period seems to have been issued under Severus Alexander (AD 222–235).

Finds from archaeological excavations indicate that Roman coins became increasingly common in Cyprus after the second century AD. It is likely that even before then the Roman denarius was the standard silver coin in use on the island, since only one issue of local silver coinage (under Vespasian) can certainly be attributed to Roman Cyprus. Other eastern silver issues, and bronzes, notably from nearby Antioch in Syria, also reached the island.

After the final cessation of local coin production early in the third century AD Cyprus relied entirely on imported coinage, even for its bronze pieces. In the course of that century the minting of local coinage came to an end throughout the Eastern Empire. A number of major provincial cities were now converted to production of Roman 'imperial' coinage as part of an empire-wide devolution of Roman coin production and issue, but Cyprus was left without a mint of its own. Thus all the coinage now going into circulation on the island had to be imported, and finds suggest that the mint of Antioch was by far the major supplier of currency to Cyprus in the late Roman Empire.

71

9 Writing

From about 1500 BC at least some Cypriots could read and write. The earliest script used in Cyprus is known as Cypro-Minoan because of its affinities with the Linear A script of Minoan Crete. Like Linear A, Cypro-Minoan is a syllabic script in which each sign represents a syllable, a combination of a consonant and a vowel. Similar too is the apparent left to right direction of the script. Neither Cypro-Minoan or Linear A have yet been deciphered, which means that we do not know what languages are transcribed. Direct relations between Cyprus and Crete were minimal at the time when Cyprus adopted the script, but it could have been passed from Crete to Cyprus in Syria, with which both had close and lively commercial relations, particularly at Ugarit. Alternatively, both Cypro-Minoan and its successor, Cypro-Syllabic, may have a common (eastern) parent. Eastern influence on Cypriot literacy is certainly evident, since the Cypriot tablets are cushion-shaped and baked in a kiln in the eastern tradition. The tablets carry continuous texts; briefer inscriptions appear on pottery vessels, clay 'balls' (whose use is unknown) and metal objects, and feature also in designs on rings and sealstones.

72 About one quarter of a cushion-shaped clay tablet inscribed on both sides in the Cypro-Minoan script. The tablet was baked in the Near Eastern tradition and one column of the original text survives. The unequal length of the lines suggest that it may be a poem, but until the script has been deciphered the meaning of the texts remains obscure. From Enkomi, *c.*1200 BC. W 9cm.

73 Marble statue base with a Greek inscription in the Greek and Cypro-Syllabic scripts which reads: 'Helloikos, the son of Poteisis dedicated this as a vow to Demeter and Kore'. From the sanctuary of Demeter at Kourion (Curium), late 4th century BC. L 28 cm.

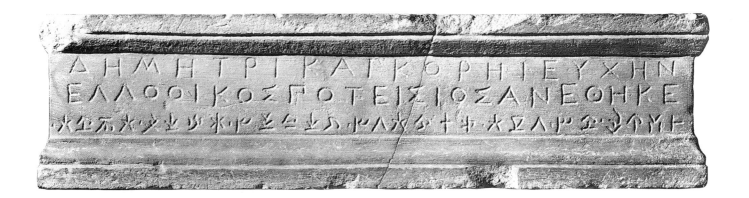

It was not until the fourteenth century BC that the script became firmly established, continuing in use for about three hundred years. Tablets (and a cylinder) with long texts have hitherto been found only at Enkomi. However, the discovery of items with brief inscriptions and bone *styli* (writing implements) at many of the other urban centres, including Kition, Hala Sultan Tekké and Old Paphos, suggest that it was widely used.

Many of the inscriptions from Iron Age Cyprus record dedications to deities or the dead, but there are a few documents referring to historical events or religious ceremonies. Inscriptions on coins name the issuing authority. The principal script in Cyprus in the earlier Iron Age was Cypro-Syllabic. It has fifty to sixty signs, each denoting a syllable and usually written from right to left, and was used to write both Greek and Eteo-Cypriot. The latter remains an unknown language and the inscriptions are undeciphered. Pre-Hellenic and pre-Semitic, the language may be the native tongue surviving from the Bronze Age. The earliest evidence for the Greek language in Cyprus is a Cypro-Syllabic inscription on a bronze spit found in a tomb at Old Paphos with grave goods dated between 1050 and 950 BC. The script was not, however, in common use until the sixth century BC. It finally died out around 200 BC. Cypro-Syllabic is apparently related to Cypro-Minoan, and also has particular affinities with the Linear B script of Mycenaean Greece. This may be partly due to the fact that both are syllabic and were used to write Greek, albeit different dialects.

74 (*Above left*) Marble statuette base with a bilingual inscription in the Cypro-Syllabic and Phoenician scripts which records a dedication to Reshef-Mikal (in the Phoenician text) or Apollo Amyklos (in the Cypro-Syllabic Greek text), by the Phoenician prince Baalröm, son of Abdimilk in the fourth year of the reign of Milkyaton, King of Kition and Idalion. This inscription assisted in the first decipherment of the Cypro-Syllabic script in the 1870s. From the sanctuary of Apollo at Idalion, early 4th century BC (the precise dates of King Milkyaton's reign are not known). W 40 cm.

Cypro-Syllabic inscriptions form two principal series, the 'normal' (or 'common') and the Paphian. The 'normal syllabary' occurs from the north-west, in the area of Marion, to the east and from north to south. This version is also used for the Eteo-Cypriot inscriptions, most of which come from Amathus and the surrounding area. The Paphian syllabary was used in both Old and New Paphos and elsewhere in the south-west, with an extension northwards. The Greek dialect of even the earliest syllabic inscription is closest to that of Arcadia in the Peloponnese. This gives some credence to the different legends that credit Arcadian Greeks with the foundation of certain Cypriot cities.

It was a 'bilingual' inscription, with Phoenician and Cypro-Syllabic on the same stone, that assisted in the first decipherment of the Cypro-Syllabic script in the 1870s by the English Assyriologist George Smith. The earliest evidence for Phoenician in Cyprus is a tomb inscription of the ninth century BC, but it is not known where it was found. From about 800 BC Phoenician inscriptions are common at Kition, as one would expect. With the spread of Phoenician influence within the island, particularly in the fifth and fourth centuries BC, the Phoenician script became more widely used. While the script only survived into the Hellenistic period, the language may have continued in use at Kition into the early Roman era. In Phoenicia itself the script had been standardised, so that it had an alphabet of twenty-two consonants by the ninth century. It was this standard form that the Phoenicians introduced to Cyprus and their other western colonies. It was also adopted and greatly improved around 750 BC by the Greeks to write their own language. About the same time it reached Italy, where it was used for Etruscan and the Italic dialects. In Cyprus, of course, the language remained Phoenician.

Cuneiform, the wedge-shaped script of western Asia, is found occasionally in Iron Age Cyprus. The most famous document is a stele erected by the Assyrian King Sargon II at Kition in 709 BC, recording the submission of the Cypriot kings. Other important documents in the cuneiform script mentioning the Cypriot kings and kingdoms have been found in the palaces of the Assyrian kings. The hieroglyphic (pictorial) script of Egypt was equally rare, but not unknown.

The Greek alphabet first appeared in Cyprus in the sixth century BC. It seems to have been officially introduced by Evagoras I at Salamis in the late fifth century; he put the Greek letter E together with the syllabary on his coins. However, it was not until a century later that the Greek alphabet became widely adopted. About 300 BC Greek inscriptions begin to outnumber those in Cypro-Syllabic. Eteo-Cypriot survived until about 219 BC, but by the end of the century the Arcado-Cypriot dialect and with it the Cypriot-Syllabic script died out. Greek became the principal script and language of Hellenistic and Roman Cyprus, as it was in the rest of the eastern Mediterranean.

Although Greek was the official language of the Roman east, Latin, the language of the ruling power, was not completely unknown in Roman Cyprus. It occurs frequently on milestones of all periods, notably at the time of the construction of the road network in the first century AD and during the major reconstruction undertaken in the early third century. The few epitaphs of Roman soldiers, a single military inscription and dedications made by Roman citizens are all, not surprisingly, written in Latin. More unusual is the Latin in architectural inscriptions and under statues dedicated to emperors at Salamis, Soloi and Chytroi, all of the first century AD. It seems that certain civic authorities were trying to find favour with the ruling power in the early years of Roman domination.

74

10 Weaponry and warfare

Around 2500 BC the first metal weapons were made and used by the Cypriots. All are of eastern types, closest perhaps to those from southern Anatolia. There are signs of unrest in the seventeenth century BC, when the number of weapons buried in cemeteries increases enormously. Several occupation sites were fortified but these, with one exception (the fortress at Nitovikla in the south of the Karpas Peninsula), are too far from the coast to have afforded protection from intruders arriving by sea. Both weapons and fortifications, therefore, are probably indications of internal strife.

The early weapon series, with hooked tangs for insertion into the handles or rivets by which they could be attached, ended in the mid-fifteenth century BC. Little is known about Cypriot weapons thereafter, until the late thirteenth and twelfth centuries BC. At that time cut-and-thrust swords were introduced from Mycenaean Greece. The type is of European origin, probably brought to the Aegean world by barbarian mercenaries hired by the Mycenaean kings. A certain type of spearhead with a socket for the handle was also of Mycenaean Greek origin. Cypriot daggers and arrowheads of this period, however, owe little to the Bronze Age Greek world and any outside inspiration must have come from the Near East. Cypriot warriors in the twelfth century were equipped with armour of Mycenaean Greek type, including helmets, greaves and shields reinforced with metal bosses. Protection for the body was provided by scale corslets of Near Eastern origin which continued to be used until the end of the sixth century BC. If the motifs on pottery imported from Mycenaean Greece in the fourteenth and thirteenth centuries BC reflect Cypriot life, it can be assumed that warriors were transported to the battlefield in horse-drawn chariots.

Iron was used in Cyprus for knives, which were secured to their handles by bronze rivets, from the mid-twelfth century BC. In the follow-

78

ing century iron became the principal material for swords and spearheads. Early iron swords are all versions of the older bronze cut-and-thrust variety. Alongside those of more modest dimensions were some impressive in their size and length. Modifications to the long sword were undertaken around 600 BC, but the persistent use of the type as late as the sixth century, shown by illustrations on vases as well as by actual finds, shows a distinct divergence from the weapons and tactics of contemporary Greece. Here a shorter sword had been introduced about 700 BC, at the time of the emergence of the hoplite *phalanx*, a formation of highly trained and well-equipped infantry. The retention of the long sword suggests that the Cypriots were rather less organised. Their armour and equipment however, were improving: shields of perishable

78

76 A bronze weapon with a hooked tang. It is long enough to have been a sword and was made between 1900 and 1650 BC. L 43.2 cm.

77 (*Left*) Terracotta model of a warrior on horseback. The horse is protected by a tasselled breast shield. The bridle has a tassle falling on to the nose and on the mane is a curving crest. The rider wears a helmet and carries a shield by a strap; 7th century BC. Ht 16.5 cm.

material were now reinforced with iron or bronze bosses, both rounded and spiked, and an all-metal spiked shield was used in the seventh century BC. Subsequently modifications to these Cypriot types were made under the influence of the Greek hoplite shield. Shields with animal head protomes were also used in Cyprus for much of the Archaic period.

Originally Assyrian, this type perhaps reached Cyprus from Urartu. It was certainly through, if not directly from, Cyprus that it became known in Crete.

Helmets in the earlier Iron Age were generally of Near Eastern varieties, but these were gradually modified under Greek influence during the later seventh and sixth centuries BC.

78 (*Left*) A copper and an iron sword of the 'cut-and-thrust' variety. The copper example (*left*) is one of a group of swords of an entirely Mediterranean type, originally of European origin and first wielded by barbarian mercenaries serving Aegean masters; from Enkomi, *c*.1150 BC. The iron sword (*right*) is the longest example of this particular type known at present. It was particularly popular in Crete, but ancestors of this weapon have also been found in Cyprus; from Amathus, *c*.7th century BC. L (of iron sword) 51.5 cm.

79 (*Above*) Terracotta figurine of a three-bodied warrior. The helmets and shields are of Cypriot type but modified under Greek influence. The breastplates are among the earliest of an innovative type combining metal (for the neckguard and arm guards) with linen or leather, suggesting that the Cypriots played a part in the development of this new type of body armour. From Pyrga, late 7th century BC. Ht 24 cm.

Protective features including a noseguard and cheekpieces, which project forward, were adopted from the Greek Corinthian type. From the late seventh century BC armour made of leather or linen with metal additions, like neckguards and shoulder-flaps, began to replace the older scale body-armour. It seems likely that Cypriot warriors played a part in the development of the Greek 'composite corslet', made of a combination of metal and linen, which was worn from the second half of the sixth century. Other items of protective armour were of Greek origin. A limestone sarcophagus of about 470/60 BC portrays Cypriot warriors with the armour and equipment of Greek hoplites. They wear Corinthian helmets, the Greek composite corslet and greaves, and carry hoplite shields and long spears. There is

also other evidence for the use of the hoplite shield in Cyprus at this time.

The Corinthian helmet was probably adopted, if not universally, towards the end of the sixth century BC. An example found in the Persian siege ramp of 498 BC at Old Paphos was apparently already a generation old when it was lost; this may have been worn by a Greek mercenary fighting on the Persian side, rather than by a Cypriot defender.

The Cypriot kings were much concerned with the fortification of their cities. As early as its foundation in the eleventh century BC Salamis had a mud-brick wall, but there is more information about the fortifications of many of the sites in the Archaic period. The walls were built of mud-brick on stone foundations. At Salamis they were now strengthened

80 Limestone sarcophagus decorated in low relief with pairs of warriors hunting animals. The warriors are dressed and equipped as Greek hoplites. They wear Corinthian helmets and Greek 'composite' corslets (breastplates of metal and linen) and are armed with hoplite shields and long thrusting spears. The sarcophagus has feet in the Cypriot tradition. Made in Cyprus, c.470–460 BC. From Golgoi. L 239.4 cm.

with casemates. At Old Paphos the wall had towers at intervals. The north-east gateway developed slowly; it started as the normal oriental type with twin bastions projecting at right angles from the city walls. The thorough-fare, 22m long and 11.8–12.7m wide, was restricted on the inside by a cross-bastion. Around 500 BC, shortly before the siege of the city by the Persians, the wall and gateway were considerably strengthened. The mud-brick faces were revetted with limestone blocks (ashlars) and a developed system of berm, ditch and glacis was provided. There was, therefore, a flat area between the wall and the ditch which had steeply sloping sides. The gateway was narrowed by cross-bastions, so as to be less than 5m wide (at the actual gate on the city side, it was only 2.9m). The cross-

bastions were arranged so that the road went through a sharp double bend and could be covered by crossfire from soldiers on the parapets. The actual gate was closed by heavy wooden doors.

Excavations have revealed the story of the Persian siege of Paphos in 498 BC. The Persians erected a huge ramp against the wall by the north-east gateway. The ramp was composed of rubble and broken limestone statues from a nearby sanctuary. On this ramp they drove up their siege engines, which acted as battering rams and firing posts. Meanwhile, the Cypriots dug long tunnels and passages from inside the wall to come up within the ramp and under the gateway. In so doing they created huge cavities propped up with beams which were finally set on fire in order to topple

81 View of the Persian siege of Old Paphos in 498 BC, after Sorrell. The Persians, whose camp is in the background, erected a huge ramp against the wall by the north-east gateway of the city. On this they drove up their siege engines, which acted as both battering rams and firing posts. The Cypriot defenders inside the city dug long tunnels and passages from inside the wall to come up within the ramp and under the gateway. Their aim was to topple the siege engines, since the tunnels and passages had created huge cavities which were propped up by beams and then finally set on fire.

the siege engines. Stone missiles were hurled from some kind of stone-throwing machine, perhaps an early catapult. Both sides fought with bows and arrows. Hundreds of arrow-heads and spearheads of bronze and iron were removed from the siege debris. Both eastern and Greek types are represented but it is impossible to know which were used by which side. It was also here that the Greek Corinthian helmet was found.

Fortifications were still important to the Cypriot kings in the Classical period. At Idalion the citadel wall of the early fifth century BC was 10.5m thick, with an inner core of small stones set in mud-mortar and faced with limestone blocks. A tower, perhaps part of a gateway, was built of fine limestone ashlars. This city withstood a siege by the Phoenicians of Kition and the Persians a generation before being captured by Kition in about the mid-fifth century BC. At Old Paphos the siege-damaged fortifications were put into a state of readiness again. The siege-ramp was surrounded by a revetment wall and included in the system. At Golgoi the fortifications of the fourth century, constructed of mud-brick on stone foundations, had houses built directly inside with their outer walls resting against the city wall, exactly as in the Greek city of Olynthus.

There is little information about the armour and weapons of Cyprus in the Hellenistic and Roman periods. That they continued along Greek lines is suggested by the discovery of a fine helmet in a tomb of about the second century BC. This is of the so-called Thracian type with scalloped cheekpieces, apparently based on a type of cap worn by the Thracians from northern Greece. Paphos, the new town founded about 320 BC by Nikokles, the last king of the city–kingdom, was immediately fortified but only its rock-cut foundations survive. An impressive rock-cut ramp led up to the north-west gateway, one of the four gates of the city, which was flanked by two rec-tangular towers. Underground chambers and passages cut into the rock close to the north gate may have housed units of the Ptolemaic garrison. The Hellenistic walls of Ayia Irini had houses built directly inside, like the fourth-century BC walls of Golgoi. The Ptole-mies made little use of Cypriot manpower, although they had a fleet based in the island in their later years. The Cypriot population was swelled by the presence of a large mercenary force. The important towns all had their own garrisons. The commander-in-chief of all the forces was second in importance to the *stragegos* (governor-general) and like him (and the majority of the company commanders) was a non-Cypriot. Many of the principal towns of Roman Cyprus, including Kition, Paphos, Curium, Lapithos, Soloi, Tamassos and, perhaps Amathus, were fortified. Some use was made of Cypriot manpower in the professional Roman army: about 2,000 were recruited at one time to serve overseas. The manufacture of a new type of arrowhead in Roman Cyprus suggests that they still fought with bows and arrows.

Although Cyprus was administered as a provincial backwater, the island's military history did not come to an end with Roman rule. During the First Jewish Revolt of AD 115–117 Cypriot Jews rose against the Roman establishment, massacring thousands of the island's non-Jewish population, and reputedly destroying the city of Salamis. The large Jewish community in the island descended from colonists who may have arrived in the late fourth century BC. The rising was ruth-lessly suppressed by Trajan's general Lusius Quietus, and Jews were forbidden in the island. In AD 269 Gothic tribes made a brief incursion, but despite these calamities the period of Roman rule in the island was relatively un-eventful, and Cyprus was able to enjoy the benefits of stability under the *pax Romana*.

82 One of originally three panels of a mosaic floor in the south-eastern side of the central court of a Roman building (a patrician's house or public baths with *palaestra*) in the city of Curium (Kourion). The mosaic depicts different stages in gladiatorial combats. The central panel illustrated here shows the gladiators fully armed and ready to strike. They are named in Greek 'Margareites' and 'Hellenikos'. Second half of the 3rd century AD.

69

Postscript

For over 7,000 years Cyprus' position in the eastern Mediterranean, at a crossroads between the major civilisations of the ancient world, had opened it to influences from many sources and had helped it to develop a unique and distinctive culture. Towards the end of this long period Cyprus was assimilated into the Hellenistic Greek world, and its own character became less distinct in the cultural sphere to which it now belonged.

The events of the fourth century AD, with the division of the Roman Empire in 395, mark the opening of a new period in Cyprus' history. During the century the island suffered drought, famine and earthquakes: in AD 342 the city of Salamis was almost entirely destroyed. Rebuilt and renamed Constantia, it replaced the old capital at New Paphos as the seat of the governor, and became the island's most important city. In AD 395 Cyprus was incorporated into the Eastern Roman Empire, and it is this period of transition that marks the end of our survey.

83 An illustration of the dramatic consequences of the devastating earthquake which destroyed Curium (Kourion) in about AD 365. The skeleton of a mule is still attached to the trough to which it had been tethered in the courtyard of a house. The trough had been hurled into the wall, tilted and cracked, while the ground beneath had subsided.

Acknowledgements

First I would like to thank Mr Constantine Leventis, Lady Hunt and other members of the Leventis family for their support in every aspect of this project. The draft text was read by Mr B.F. Cook, Professor F.G. Maier and Dr Susan Woodford and I am indebted to them for their helpful comments and suggestions. My particular thanks are due also to Ms J. Lesley Fitton, Dr R.S. Merrillees, Dr Martin Price and Miss Louise Schofield and to Dr Ian Carradice for chapter 8. For advice on more specific points I am most grateful to Miss Carol Andrews, Mr D.M. Bailey, Professor J. Boardman, Dr Diana Buitron, Professor J.N. Coldstream, Dr P.T. Craddock, Dr Elizabeth Goring, Miss Hero Granger-Taylor, Dr M. Henig, Dr Maria Iakovou, Mr I.D. Jenkins, Professor O. Masson, Dr Ellen Macnamara, Mr G. Markoe, Dr E.J. Peltenburg, Mr A. Reyes, Dr R. Senff, Dr D. Soren, Dr Judith Swaddling, Dr S. Swiny and Dr D.J.R. Williams. The Director of the Department of Antiquities of Cyprus, Dr Vassos Karageorghis, and all the Staff have given their full co-operation. Many of my colleagues have helped in the production of this book. I am indebted to them all, especially Mrs Marian Vian for typing the text, Miss Susan Bird for the maps and drawing of the siege and Miss Jane Beamish, Mr P. Gardner and Mr P.E. Nicholls of the British Museum Photographic Service. I would also like to thank British Museum Publications Ltd, in particular the editor, Miss Jenny Chattington, and Miss Celia Clear. Finally I must thank my children, Hugh (6½), Miranda (4) and Lucy (2½) for keeping rather quieter than usual during the writing of this book and my husband, Tim, for helping them achieve this.

Veronica Tatton-Brown
July 1987

Further reading

References to books and articles on specific topics will be found in some of the general works listed here.

A.C. Brown and H.W. Catling, *Ancient Cyprus* (revised edn, Oxford 1986)

B.F. Cook (ed.), *Cypriote Art in the British Museum* (London 1979)

Sir George Hill, *A History of Cyprus* vols I–IV (Cambridge 1948–1952)

Sir David Hunt (ed.), *Footprints in Cyprus* (London 1982)

V. Karageorghis, *Cyprus, from the Stone Age to the Romans* (London 1982)

V. Karageorghis (ed.), *Archaeology in Cyprus 1960–1985* (Nicosia 1985)

F.G. Maier *Cypern. Insel am Kreuzweg der Geschichte* (2nd edn, Munich 1982)

F.G. Maier and V. Karageorghis, *Paphos. History and Archaeology* (Nicosia 1984)

Desmond Morris, *The Art of Ancient Cyprus* (Oxford 1985)

V. Tatton-Brown (ed.), *Cyprus BC: 7,000 Years of History* (London 1979)

Photo acknowledgements

Vassos Karageorghis contents page
Veronica Tatton-Brown 1, 61
Xenophon Michael 20, 34, 48, 57, 72, back cover
Department of Antiquities of Cyprus 4, 8
M.L. Katzev 21
T.W.T. Tatton-Brown 63, 82
Metropolitan Museum of Art (Cesnola Collection, purchased by subscription 1874–1876) 80
David Soren 83

British Museum registration and catalogue numbers of objects illustrated

Numbers are given in the order in which objects are described in the picture captions.

Front cover
BM Cat. Sculpture C 154
Inside front cover
BM Cat. Jewellery 1646–7
Title page
BM Cat. Terracottas A 43

Fig
2 BM Cat. Jewellery 194, 102
3 BM Cat. G & R Glass 14
5 BM Cat. Terracottas A 188, A 182, A 225
6 BM Cat. Vases C 134
7 GR 1929.2–11.2
9 BM Cat. Vases C 732
10 GR 1897.4–1.300
11 GR 1873.3–20.339
12 BM Cat. Sculpture C 352
13 BMC Cyprus 22
14 GR 1979.12–14.1
15 GR 1920.12–20.1
16 GR 1872.8–16.98
17 BM Cat. Bronzes 111, 107, 112
18 GR 1903.12–15.48
19 GR 1876.9–9.112
22 a) BM Cat. Vases C 71; b) GR 1939.2–17.71; c) BM Cat. Vases C 64
23 a) GR 1884.12–10.69; b) GR 1981.12–18.53
24 a) GR 1985.10–8.1; b) BM Cat. Vases C 252
25 GR 1897.4–1.999
26 GR 1911.4–28.1
27 GR 1897.4–1.996
28 GR 1927.12–13.2
29 BM Cat. Vases C 855, C 1025
30 BM Cat. Vases C 974
31 BM Cat. Vases C 904
32 a) BM Cat. G & R Glass 364; b) BM Cat. Vases C 940; c) GR 1881.8–24.70; d) BM Cat. Lamps Q 500; e) GR 1881.8–24.50
33 a) BM Cat. Lamps Q 2453; b) GR 1908.4–11.10; c) GR 1896.2–1.298; d) GR 1872.7–26.6; e) GR 1876.9–9.40; f) GR 1884.12–10.258; g) GR 1888.11–12.1; h) BM Cat. Lamps Q 2580; i) GR 1876.9–9.47
35 On loan from the Old Palace School, Croydon
36 BM Cat. Vases C 303, C 311, C 261, C 302
37 BM Cat. Terracottas A 16, A 15
38 BM Cat. Vases C 838
39 GR 1910.6–20.1
40 BM Cat. Sculpture C 12
41 BM Cat. 1873.3–20.87
42 BM Cat. Sculpture C 131
43 BM Cat. Sculpture C 321
44 BM Cat. Terracottas A 406, A 410
45 BM Cat. Sculpture 1992
46 a) BM Cat. Jewellery 779–80; b) Jewellery 299–300; c) GR 1897.4–1.208, 209; d) Jewellery 623; e) Jewellery 580
47 BM Cat. Jewellery 552, 550
49 BM Cat. Gems 527, 481
50 BM Cat. Jewellery 2053, 1728–9, 1958
51 BM Cat. Finger Rings a) 1641; b) 175; c) 1242; d) 851
52 BM Cat. Jewellery a) 2407–8; b) 2526–7; c) 2723
53 GR 1929.10–14.1
54 BM Cat. Terracottas A 123
55 BM Cat. Terracottas A 150, A 151
56 BM Cat. Sculpture C 216
58 a) BM Cat. Terracottas A 84; b) BM Cat. Sculpture C 30; c) Sculpture C 242
59 BM Cat. Sculpture C 164
60 BMC Cyprus 62
62 BM Cat. Sculpture C 429
64 BM Cat. Paintings 8
65 BM Cat. Sculpture C 431
66 1871.17–1.1
67 a) BMC Salamis 23; b) BMC Paphos 39; c) BMC Citium 6
68 a) BMC Salamis 51; b) BMC Salamis 53; c) BMC Salamis 54; d) 1920.3–26.9
69 1873.8–3.1; R. Payne Knight Bequest
70 BMC Cleopatra 2
71 BMC Cyprus 22
72 BM Cat. Greek Inscriptions 968a
74 WAA 125.320
75 BM Cat. Jewellery 1999
76 GR 1969.12–31.100
77 GR 1876.9–9.91
78 BM Cat. Bronzes 72; GR 1894.11–1.689
79 GR 1866.1–1.298 and 299

Index